THE SEA ANGLER IN IRELAND

THE SEA
ANGLER IN IRELAND

BY KEN WHELAN

FOREWORD BY JACK CHARLTON

COUNTRY HOUSE

Published by
Country House
41 Marlborough Road
Donnybrook
Dublin 4
Ireland

First published in 1989 as part of
The Angler in Ireland: Game, Coarse & Sea.

This edition published in 1991.
© Ken Whelan 1989, 1991

British Library Cataloguing in Publication Data
Whelan, Ken *1951-*
    The sea angler in Ireland.
    1. Ireland. Angling
    I. Title
    799.1209415

ISBN 0-946172-24-2

Managing editor: Treasa Coady
Illustrator and designer: Bill Murphy
Photography: Mike Bunn
Text editors: Elaine Campion, Siobhán Parkinson
Typeset by Printset & Design Ltd, Dublin
Colour separation by Kulor Centre, Dublin
Printed in Hong Kong

CONTENTS

ACKNOWLEDGEMENTS

To acknowledge all of those who contributed to this book would be an almost impossible task; for angling books are never really original works, they are a distillation of experiences, thoughts, conversations and views. To attribute to each friend or acquaintance their rightful credit is patently impossible. All I can do is to thank those who have contributed directly to the production of the final work and to collectively acknowledge my gratitude to the many other anglers and friends who have influenced my thinking on angling over the years.

First and foremost I must thank 'the team' who contributed generously and enthusiastically to the book and its creation: Treasa Coady, my publisher; Bill Murphy, illustrator and designer; Mike Bunn, photographer; Elaine Campion and Siobhán Parkinson, copy editors; and to Phil Browne who did such an excellent job in typing and formatting the original text.

To the many people who provided original technical material for inclusion in the book, and to all of those who took so much trouble in facilitating photographic sessions, particularly those whose patience was sorely tried by the vagaries of the weather and the photographer's craft. The manuscript was read and objectively criticised by a range of specialists, whose incisive comments have greatly improved the technical precision of the text; none the less, any remaining errors or omissions are my own.

I am grateful to the following for permission to use passages from their publications: The Central Fisheries Board; Bord Fáilte; David and Charles Ltd; Sidgwick and Jackson.

A special word of thanks must go to my parents and family, especially my father and my brother Brendan, constant angling companions for over thirty years, who have helped to make so many angling dreams come true. Their patience, interest and active support in all of my 'mad cap' schemes is rarely articulated but much appreciated.

Finally and most importantly, to my dear wife Frances, for all of the sacrifices she has made to ensure the completion of the book, particularly her patience and ingenuity in keeping the family amused while I scribbled away incessantly for almost a year; to my children David and Laura without whom the text would have been completed in half the time but whose very existence has made the whole project so worthwhile.

Ken Whelan
Newport, Co. Mayo
March 1991

FOREWORD

One of the many perks which came with my job as manager of the Irish soccer team was the opportunity to sample the range and quality of angling available in Ireland. And what splendid fishing there is — the magnificent pollack and coalfish, the powerful tope, blue and porbeagle shark, and the ubiquitous shoals of hard-fighting mullet and mackerel. I could go on and on. Most of all, compared to the crowded British and continental waters, the anglers are few and far between. I enjoy fishing in Ireland, and I know a lot of anglers who are only now discovering Ireland as an angling destination.

Now, at last, there is a comprehensive book on all forms of sea angling in Ireland. This is not just a guide to Irish angling or a 'how-to-do-it' manual, it is a great read for anglers anywhere. Ken combines his passion for angling with his training as a scientist. The result is that rare combination — a scientist who can communicate the latest knowledge about fish and fishing in a fascinating and readable way. I love to learn about the behaviour and habits of my quarry and I found this aspect of the book particularly absorbing. It is in no way a dry or difficult text and the photography is great. It combines biological insights with sound advice on tackle and descriptions of methods and locations, with many amusing stories and scenes culled from a lifetime of fish chasing.

This book will be read with pleasure and profit by anglers everywhere, but those visiting Ireland from abroad will particularly benefit from it. The specialist will appreciate the detailed advice on locations, tackle and local methods while the beginner will find the author's sound common sense an invaluable guide in his early efforts. I hope the book will encourage visitors to 'have a go' and fish for species that they do not usually catch at home. Such angling opportunities abound in Ireland and are within easy reach of every major angling centre.

I can heartily recommend this book — I hope other anglers can get from it some of the benefit and pleasure it has given me.

Jack Charlton
Dalton, March 1991

INTRODUCTION

For an island people we Irish have made little real use of the seas around us and for historical reasons have no great tradition of seafaring. Saint Brendan, who, it is said, discovered America before Christopher Columbus, was an obvious exception. But we are not a maritime nation in the same sense as the Faroese or the Icelanders who for centuries have travelled over hundreds, or indeed thousands, of miles of ocean in search of migrating stocks of fish. We had for centuries little contact with the ocean except when crossing it in search of a better future in foreign lands.

Little wonder then that sea angling, that most wondrous of sports, had few native devotees before the advent of those great deep sea anglers, the Dreadnoughts, into Ballycotton around the turn of the century. The massive skate, ling, conger and shark which these maritime merlins conjured up from the depths of the ocean were a cause of wonderment and disbelief to the local populations. Those old enough to remember still speak in hushed tones and with reverence about those great angling days. The catches are always referred to as 'creatures' or 'great animals' but never fish. It is as if, in the eyes of the locals, the visitors had perpetrated some heinous crime by extracting from the depths of the ocean creatures which were destined by God to remain hidden and concealed from view forever.

At the turn of this century Ireland was, in fish terms, similar to the Alaska of today. It had largely escaped the ravages of the industrial revolution and fish abounded in its pollution-free lakes, rivers and streams, and in its totally unexploited seas. Rod catches of sea fish were measured in fractions of a ton, trout by the dozen and seasonal salmon catches in thousands of pounds.

The visiting angler

In order to be successful, it is very important that visiting anglers have a real appreciation of the present state of angling in Ireland. It is true that, comparatively speaking, Ireland has arguably the finest variety of angling available anywhere in Europe. It can still boast great lake fisheries which are as yet uncharted and some of the finest wild brown trout fishing to be found anywhere in the world.

However, like many other developing countries, Ireland's fisheries have suffered at the hands of so-called industrial and agricultural progress. The problems facing Irish angling must be contrasted with the vast resource which remains unscathed by modern-day advances. Ireland is a sparsely populated country with the majority of its people centred either along its Eastern coastline or in large urban centres.

Using this book

If the angler is to be successful on his first visit to Ireland he must do two things: he must carefully choose the water or waters to be fished and have a comprehensive knowledge of his quarry and the most up-to-date methods used in its capture.

The main purpose of this book is to provide the angler with a comprehensive review of the species which he is likely to encounter while fishing in Ireland, to give some biological facts on the various species and to list the modern methods of capturing each species or group of fish.

I firmly believe that the more successful angler is the one who appreciates the basic behavioural biology of his quarry and can make intelligent decisions regarding the reaction of his quarry to various environmental conditions.

It is obviously not possible to include in one volume all of the specialist information which is available on any given species. The reader will, however, be referred to other articles and books containing such material, should he wish to expand his knowledge of any one species of fish.

Most holiday anglers will find time during their stay in Ireland to explore new waters and to experiment with new types of angling. They will be pleasantly surprised by the variety of species available within easy reach of their chosen centre. Such a choice of species may become even more important during periods of adverse weather conditions. For instance, the deep sea angler who is blown off the sea may find the prospect of a day's trout or salmon fishing most inviting. Conversely, the salmon angler who is faced, day after day, by a drought-ridden river may find that his days are better spent hunting for ray, pollack or coalfish in neighbouring bays, leaving the evenings and early mornings free to concentrate on his primary quarry.

The book is intended for those who have a basic knowledge of angling and no effort is made to give instructions on basic techniques such as casting.

Measurements are given in both their imperial and metric forms, except in the case of metres and kilometres where only the metric form is used. The metric conversions are intended only as a guide and are generally rounded to the nearest half unit. One measure which continental anglers may not be familiar with is the 'fathom' (fm); it is used to express ocean depths (1fm = 1.83m).

In general there is a great deal of nonsense talked about the 'proper' tackle and the limitations of using a general set of all-purpose equipment. When one considers that the fish generally sees, at most, no more than 1 to 3ft (30–90cm) of the terminal tackle, it matters little to him what type of rod, reel or indeed angler is attached to the other end of the equipment. In this book, therefore,

I concentrate on the most up-to-date terminal rigs for each type of fishing, and although the ideal equipment is described, the dilettante angler is advised on how best to adapt his tackle to suit a given situation. Obviously, there are limits to such adaptation but generally where really specialised or particularly strong equipment is required, it can be hired locally (eg deep sea fishing).

Although I have attempted to lighten each chapter through the inclusion of anecdotes and fishermen's stories, my book remains above all a fishing manual. The readers will notice that, throughout the text, fish are referred to as 'he' rather than 'it'. This is a standard convention in angling writing; the pronoun is used in an asexual sense to personalise the relationship between the angler and the fish. Its use is not intended, in any way, to degrade or denigrate the female of the species.

It is my earnest hope that the readers will benefit over time from this book; that their bags will increase in both weight and variety as a result, and that it will encourage them to experiment with new species and new fishing environments so that they too can gain even a fraction of the enjoyment which Irish angling has given me over the past thirty years.

NOTE: On occasions throughout this book, cross-references are made. The page numbers given refer to the original edition, that is, The Angler in Ireland: Game, Coarse & Sea **(Country House, 1989). Such references should be ignored.**

CHAPTER 1

A BRIEF HISTORY

The Ballycotton Fishery

It was a cold stormy May afternoon and the strong south-east gale was lashing with all of its pent up fury against the exposed beach. Great rows of crashing white-topped breakers were assaulting the base of the sand dunes as flocks of storm-bound sea birds half rose from the land, testing the wind's strength. Blown back onto the strand, they joined their earthbound companions who picked and pecked impatiently at the barren sand and from time to time at one another.

As I rounded the corner into the town itself, I was immediately struck by the majestic island-bound lighthouse which lay just off the mainland. Its craggy perimeter was a mass of seething foam as the breakers tried, with all their power, to topple the gaunt, vivid white tower and life-saving beacon.

This was Ballycotton, seminal home of Irish sea angling; the town which has played welcoming host to so many famous sea anglers for almost a century. Had the fishing changed over the years? Were the legendary monsters of the deep still lurking in the neighbouring seas? Had commercial fishing reduced the abundance of larger fish?

Two hours later I had the answer to these and many other questions. My hosts for the afternoon were Peter Manning, a local skipper and co-manager with Dietmar Scharf of the Ballycotton Angling Centre, and Ann Flynn, proprietor of the Bay View Hotel. Ann's hotel has catered for sea anglers since 1909 and she has in her possession a set of unique record books and photographs dating from the arrival of the first pioneering British sea anglers. A neighbouring hotel, Fawcett's, also catered for anglers during those early years but unfortunately all their records were destroyed in a tragic fire many years ago.

The British Sea Anglers' Society

Irish sea angling was really a British invention; for it was members of the British Sea Anglers' Society who first discovered its staggering potential in the early years of this century.

The British Sea Anglers' Society was a most interesting group of individuals. Founded in 1893, its original membership and list of patrons reads like a Who's Who of the British peerage of the time. The society's fashionable club premises were situated at 4 Fetters Lane, Fleet Street, where, in addition to meeting rooms, an extensive library and museum were quickly established. The members met each Wednesday evening and produced a fine quarterly journal containing all the up-to-date information a sea angler could require: tides, bait locations, fishing locations, contacts, etc. Interestingly, all the information was supplied to members on the basis that it would remain confidential. The society also formulated separate specimen fish weight categories for both shore and boat and organised a series of annual competitions, including a specific competition restricted to Irish waters.

Soon after the establishment of the society, members began to catalogue the best sea fishing locations in the British Isles and realised that little was known about Ireland (then part of the British empire). Exploratory trips to locations such as Courtmacsherry, County Cork, Waterville, County Kerry, and of course Ballycotton, County Cork, provided unsurpassed sport and soon these centres became the bulwark of their Irish involvement.

The Dreadnought Sea Angling Society

As the British Sea Anglers' Society gradually spread its attentions further and further afield and as its members encountered new and exotic sport fish, it was decided that the society required a name which would epitomise its fearless, undauntable spirit — hence its now famous new title of the Dreadnought Sea Angling Society.

The Bay View records show that the Dreadnoughts enjoyed some exceptional fishing. Now uncommon species such as large halibut and skate (or 'scate', as they are frequently described in the records) were plentiful and they also tangled with large ling, pollack, cod, conger, tope and blue shark. Surprisingly, however, with the exception of skate and halibut, the quantities and size of species available to the angler in Ballycotton has remained stable over the years. According to Peter Manning, the rough, inhospitable ground has preserved the deep sea angling in an almost pristine condition. Ballycotton's shore angling is also of the highest calibre and to prove the point, Eddie Cull, a local man, holds no fewer than four Irish records (black sole, plaice, homelyn and painted ray), all taken from the shore — surely a record in itself.

Fortunately, some of the Dreadnoughts were meticulous diarists and they have recorded in great detail their good and bad fishing expeditions. Yes, even in those days, bad weather and poor mackerel stocks were frequently blamed for the poor standard of fishing.

When the rather primitive tackle used by the early Dreadnoughts and the meagre information then available on the more common species are taken into account, their success is truly outstanding. For example, in 1914, G. E. Merrin of Surrey records the following catch in a little over three weeks:

Date: 3 June 1914 to 27/6/14 Boatman: Tom Sullivan
Name: G. E. Merrin Where Fishing: No Sunday Fishing and 1 day bad weather

Merrin 2469½lbs [1120kg] 37. Specimen Fish.
Weight with partners 3310lb [1501kg], including
Skate 91lbs [41kg]
1 Ling 42½lbs [19kg]
1 Pollack 14lbs [6kg]
1 Halibut 48½lbs [22kg] Ellis
1 Blue Shark 78lbs [35kg] Merrin
1 Cod 28lbs [13kg] ''

By the early 1930s the Dreadnoughts had become truly efficient in their chosen sport. Throughout the 1930s a party led by an F. Clark visited the Bay View. Mr Clark, in a meticulously clear hand, records every detail of each trip, and some were impressively fruitful. For example, a thirteen-day trip in 1934 produced a total of 7680½lb (3500kg) of fish! I have reproduced here details of that trip exactly as laid down by the good Mr Clark:

Date: Sept. 1st-12th Boatman: Lynch, P. Sliney, Murphy
Tide: 1st week dead slack Wind: Mainly N.W.
   2nd Fair Tide Weather: Marvellous.
Name: F. Clarke, W. Clark, W. Medcalf, Where Fishing: East & West.
   T. Munyard & G. Gladding & F. Land (1 week).
Catch Total 7680½lbs [3500kg]

Individual Catches

A. Holland	1588½ lbs	[721kg]
W. Clark	1209½ lbs	[549kg]
F. Clark	1160½ lbs	[526kg]
S. Morris	1013 lbs	[460kg]
W. S. Medcalf	936½ lbs	[428kg]
B. Black	582¾ lbs	[310kg]
T. Munyard	554½ lbs	[252kg]
G. Gladding	476 lbs	[216kg]
F. Land	59¼ lbs	[27kg]

Best Special Fish

W. Clark	Bream	4 lbs	[2kg]
	Scate	155 lbs	[70kg]
	Conger	48 lbs	[22kg]
	Cod	22 lbs	[10kg]
	Pollack	13 lbs	[6kg]
	Ling	24 lbs	[11kg]
F. Clark	Pollack	10½ lbs	[5 kg]
	Scate	104 lbs	[47kg]
	Ling	29 lbs	[13kg]
	Bream	4 lbs	[2kg]
	Cod	20 lbs	[9kg]
R. Black	Bream	4 lbs	[2kg]
	Pollack	12 lbs	[6kg]
	Cod	30 lbs	[14kg]
A. Holland	Ling	26 lbs	[12kg]
	Scate	108 lbs	[49kg]
	Blue Shark	33 lbs	[15kg]
	Pollack	13 lbs	[6kg]
	Bream	4¼ lbs	[2kg]
W. Medcalf	Scate	112 lbs	[51kg]
	Pollack	10 lbs	[5kg]
	Cod	23 lbs	[10kg]
	Ling	22 lbs	[10kg]
S. Morris	Scate	108 lbs	[49kg]
	Ling	26 lbs	[11kg]
	Bream	4 lbs	[2kg]
	Tope	31 & 33 lbs	[14 & 15kg]
	Pollack	12 lbs	[5kg]
	Cod	15 lbs	[7kg]

13 days' fishing 3 tons 8½cwt.

A 114lb common skate, taken from Fenit pier, Co. Kerry, by Michael Latchford (on right) in April 1961 (Photo courtesy CFB)

A 109lb halibut taken from the Ballycotton grounds in 1951

Clark's catch was not exceptional, for there is also a record some two years later of a party taking 8045lb (3700kg) of fish in only fifteen days. The Bay View diaries are also high in their praise of the service and hospitality shown by their boatmen; families such as the Sullivans, Slineys and Welches are frequently mentioned. Modern records show that this traditional homeliness has been lovingly and jealously maintained by the people of Ballycotton.

Big game anglers

Also during the 1930s, resident Irish anglers were beginning to experiment with new forms of big game angling. Amongst the forerunners were Dr O'Donnell Brown and the Marquis of Sligo, who set themselves the task of taking, on rod and line, the great battling porbeagle shark which frequented the waters around Achill Island in the west of Ireland. Using tackle similar to that shown in the Ballycotton photographs and fishing out of small 5.5m open wooden boats, they succeeded in landing substantial numbers of these great beasts. They were also the first to use rubby-dubby (see page 359) in Ireland. They continued to set themselves higher and higher weight targets, until they achieved the elusive 300lb (136kg) mark. The crowning glory of their achievements was the capture, on 28 September 1932, by O'Donnell Brown, of a 365lb (166kg) porbeagle; that fish still holds the official Irish record for the species.

Sea-angling clubs

Throughout the 1940s, sea angling was largely confined to a handful of small but enthusiastic clubs. Chief amongst these was the Knights of the Silver Hook, a Dublin-based club, founded in 1913, which formed the foundation stone of native interest in the sport.

The credit for first attempting to organise sea angling on a national basis must go to Captain Maurice Dalton. A founder member of a group titled the Irish Sea Anglers' Society, he proposed, in 1942, that all the main commercial ports and traditional sea angling centres be circulated with a view to stimulating an interest in sea angling, both as a sport and as a potential tourist attraction. Sadly, his attempts came to nothing.

It was ten years later, in November 1953, that a second attempt was made to gather together the disparate groups interested in sea angling. The initiative was stimulated by overtures which were made by the Knights of the Silver Hook to General Hugo McNeill, the founder and administrator of An Tostal, for sponsorship. An Tostal was a concept designed to stimulate an interest and an appreciation in all things Irish by means of festivals, seminars and competitions. The Knights were told that sea angling could only be included if it was represented by a national group but that bronze plaques would be made available to such a national umbrella group.

The Irish Federation of Sea Anglers

On that afternoon of Sunday 29 November 1953 representatives from six sea angling clubs met in the Central Hotel, Dublin, to discuss the formation of an Irish Federation of Sea Anglers, to consider a draft of a proposed constitution to govern the federation, to arrange for a first general meeting to be held in early 1954 to ratify the constitution, and to elect a committee for the year 1954. Maurice Dalton was responsible for arranging the meeting and it was he who prepared a draft constitution and rules. Representatives from Bangor Sea Angling Club, Belfast Waltonians' Angling Society, Dún Laoghaire Sea Anglers' Association, Knights of the Silver Hook Sea Angling Club, Kinsale Sea Angling Club and Shannon Airport Angling Society attended. Amongst those present at the inaugural meeting were Captains Christy O'Toole and Paddy Saul. These two men between them, through the aegis of the fledgling Irish Federation of Sea Anglers, were to profoundly influence modern sea angling in Ireland.

The first AGM of the federation was held on 24 April 1954 at the Lios Mara Hotel, Dún Laoghaire. At the meeting, Paddy Saul was elected chairman, Maurice Dalton vice-chairman, and Christy O'Toole secretary. The six clubs listed earlier were officially affiliated to the federation at that first AGM.

The fifties was the era of Paddy Saul and Christy O'Toole, for throughout the decade the two men worked tirelessly organising clubs throughout the length and breadth of the country. When functional, clubs were then officially affiliated to the expanding federation. Evenings, long weekends, and even summer holidays were selflessly sacrificed to the task in hand, and the work prospered.

Parallel developments

In parallel with the work of the federation, certain sea angling centres within the country were mobilising themselves and working closely with the various bodies concerned with the development and promotion of sea angling.

Westport was one of the first such groups, and under the leadership of a most able and progressive organising committee, it had, within a matter of a few short years, established itself as one of the key sea angling centres in Europe. The fishing in Westport was truly exceptional and its reputation was largely based on a good stock of large monkfish and excellent populations of large ray (7-14lb; 3-6kg).

The appointment of an organiser/adviser

It must be admitted that the timing of these developments was most opportune. The Inland Fisheries Trust, under the able and innovative direction of Michael Kennedy, was assisting the federation in its work and generally influencing official attitudes towards sea angling. Its tourism potential was now being recognised and increasing levels of state funding were being made available for the promotion of Irish angling. This culminated on 1 April 1958 with the appointment of Des Brennan as full-time sea angling organiser/adviser to the Inland Fisheries Trust; so began a whole new era in the development of Irish sea angling.

After three weeks of background reading and research in the Trust's offices in Westmoreland Street, Dublin, each day anxiously awaiting instructions, it became clear to Des that there were no formal instructions forthcoming; the concept was clear, organise and expand Irish sea angling, but the methodology was to be of his own making. With the determination and initiative that was to mark his thirty-year career in fisheries, he set to the task.

Loading all the necessary equipment into the back of his Bedford car, Des headed to the coast and for the next decade was rarely away from it for longer than a week or two. As his brief dictated, he worked closely with Bord Fáilte and the federation, indeed either Paddy or Christy continued to accompany him on his many visits to new centres. There they would earmark key individuals and with their assistance, form a club which would subsequently be affiliated to the federation. Many of the groups were not sea angling clubs in the modern sense, but rather development groups who saw sea angling as a key basis for expanding tourism in their areas. Many of these groups, such as Kinsale, later expanded into fully fledged tourism development groups, leaving the original sea angling club to the genuine anglers.

Bord Fáilte

Bord Fáilte greatly assisted in this work through the provision of funds for boats and for promotion, where required. In hindsight, the Bord Fáilte scheme for grant-aiding boats, although well intentioned, was weak on several fronts. Grants were given to large numbers of single boats rather than ensuring that at least four to five suitable boats were available in each centre, on the assumption that one successful operation in a port would stimulate interest amongst other fishermen. However, since one operator could only deal with a tiny clientele (four to six people per day, at most), the initiative never really fully succeeded. Boat sizes were also too small in that the skipper of an angling boat has a very confined season in Ireland and being realistic, requires a craft capable of carrying out small-time commercial fishing during the off-season. This concept seemed to be anathema to Bord Fáilte at the time.

Team competitions

On the promotion front, it was decided that the only effective way of highlighting Irish angling was by organising selected groups of influential British anglers to visit the country on a low-cost basis. Through Leslie Hastillow, of the National Federation of Sea Anglers in Britain, team

Four generations of Irish sea angling: (left to right) John O'Brien, founder member of the Irish Match Angling and Surfcasting Association (IMASA); Des Brennan (now retired) of the central Fisheries Board; Captain Christy O'Toole, founder member of the Irish Federation of Sea Anglers; and Kevin Linnane of the Central Fisheries Board

competitions were organised in Ireland. Teams consisted of four individuals, each representing a different angling club. Bord Fáilte paid for their travel and accommodation while Des Brennan handled the groups, arranged the actual angling events and subsequently wrote articles in the angling press covering the events. These team competitions proved to be a resounding success. They also had valuable side benefits in that the British anglers chosen were accomplished shore anglers, an area where Irish anglers were particularly weak. They brought with them for the first time such revolutionary tackle as cane beachcasters and multiplier reels.

Des also made valuable contacts through the angling press and soon names such as Clive Gammon, Hugh Stoker, Mike Prichard and Brian Harris became synonymous with the promotion of Irish angling. Although the publicity surrounding boat angling covered a variety of species, the shore angling was principally concerned with one species and one species only, the bass. It was understandable, for at that time Ireland boasted some of the finest bass fishing to be found anywhere in Europe.

As interest grew in sea angling as a viable basis for more broadly based tourism initiatives, so did the funding which Bord Fáilte was willing to commit on its promotion. Fortunately, this awareness came at a time of plenty, when the economy of the Republic was booming.

Individual experiments

While all of these exciting developments were taking place on a national basis, a unique series of experiments was in progress off the west coast of Clare. Jack Shine, a local creamery manager, set himself the task of taking 100lb+ porbeagle shark from the shore. Fishing an area known as Green Island, situated on the southern corner of Liscannor Bay, Jack succeeded in taking shark of 77lb, 75lb and 91lb (35, 34 and 41kg) during his first season, 1962.

During the following, 1963, season Jack took two exceptional shark of 130lb (60kg) and 138lb (62.5kg) and the following season he pushed his record even higher, landing two porbeagle of 140 and 145lb (63.5, 66kg). Although he subsequently set himself a target of 200lb (91kg) this ambition was not realised.

It is with the appointment of a protègè of Jack's, Kevin Linnane of Lahinch, County Clare, to the staff of the Inland Fisheries Trust, that we rejoin the mainstream of sea angling development. Kevin was appointed in 1966 to assist Des Brennan in his work and he largely assumed Des's survey role, updating and improving on previously scarce information regarding the lesser known areas. He compiled the data in the form of detailed sea angling maps which are still in use today. His proud boast is that he has visited every accessible beach around the Irish coast at least three times!

The Finola

Soon after Kevin's appointment it was decided that the IFT could no longer rely on the hire of boats for their work, particularly the valuable research work which was being carried out under the supervision of Michael Kennedy. A research boat named the *Finola* was purchased and officially launched on 4 June 1970.

She was fashioned from a 10m fibreglass hull and was powered by twin 75hp Volvo Penta inboard/outboard engines. Her cruising speed was 22km/hr and she had a range of 680km. She had ample accommodation for four and, if required, could stay at sea for several days.

A selection of modern fixed-spool and multiplier reels is offset by a traditional centre-pin reel

The *Finola* was staffed by a multicoloured crew, including Peter Brown, Peter Green, and the skipper, Kevin Linnane. For the following four years it carried out invaluable survey and tagging work around the coast. Amongst the species tagged were blue shark, porbeagle shark, ray, skate, tope and monkfish. It was as a result of this tagging programme that those in authority began to realise that certain valuable stocks such as monkfish, skate and ray were exceptionally sedentary and localised.

Developments within the Irish Federation of Sea Anglers

But what of the Irish Federation of Sea Anglers? It had truly prospered during the intervening years and by the mid-sixties had grown to such an extent that four regional councils and a governing central council were established. Tragically, Paddy Saul passed away quite unexpectedly during 1968 but the senior committee members, under the able leadership of Christy O'Toole, rallied round and in the reorganisation, Christy took over the mantle of chairman.

Throughout the remaining years of the seventies, the federation continued to grow and prosper and it represented almost 200 registered clubs by 1980. As the federation grew larger it became, dare I say, a little complacent regarding its role as mentor and competition organiser. But this too was soon to change.

Irish Match Angling and Surfcasting Association (IMASA)

In the early eighties a group calling itself the Killoughter Specimen Hunters was formed. This club was manned by a collection of fit progressive young men whose principal aim was to devise and adapt modern sea angling techniques and to apply these to shore angling. As they achieved their various ambitions regarding the capture of targeted species of fish, their competitive spirit turned them, understandably, towards competition fishing.

To further their ambitions in this regard, they formed a club known as the Irish Match Angling and Surfcasting Association (IMASA). The founding members of IMASA were John O'Brien, David Grey, Mick Dixon and Mick Kearney. The principal aims of the association were: to update match fishing rules and conditions; to ensure that competition times and venues were carefully chosen so as to optimise the return to the angler; and to introduce a more professional and organised approach to the administration of matches.

Since its inception in 1983, IMASA has certainly revolutionised the whole gambit of sea angling competition fishing in Ireland. The introduction of zoning shore competitions run on strict conservation principles and the generous sponsorship of major matches have greatly assisted in lifting the profile of sea angling amongst the general public. Irish sea angling matches are now highly organised, well-administered affairs which run throughout all seasons of the year and often attract well over 200 entrants per competition. During 1987 IMASA handled over IR£12 000 in prize funds.

IMASA's whole approach to competitive fishing ran contrary to some senior committee members' views within the federation, particularly the introduction of cash prizes into sea angling matches. The age old dispute regarding the thin line between amateurism and professionalism, which has bedevilled so many sports, ran riot for several years and attempts were even made to ban IMASA from membership of the federation.

Thankfully, common sense has now prevailed and both parties have learned to live amicably with one another. It did require compromise from both sides but as a result, we now have in Ireland a match fishing circuit comparable with that available anywhere else in Europe, and I am convinced that Irish teams will, in the future, figure prominently in international competitions.

Central and Regional Fisheries Boards

The work of updating survey material, producing guide books and articles and assisting with the general development and promotion of sea angling continues today on a national basis. It is now the responsibility of the Central and Regional Fisheries Boards who, in conjunction with Bord Fáilte, have recently compiled a list of prime branded centres which will be selectively marketed. A series of five regionally based sea angling guides have also been produced by the boards' two able sea angling officers, Peter Green and Norman Dunlop. Overall, the future prospects for Irish sea angling are excellent, provided that competing commercial fisheries are contained or reduced.

CHAPTER 2

THE MARINE RESOURCE

The freshwater angler who turns his attentions to the sea has a great deal to learn. When taken seriously, sea angling is enveloped by a different ethos, everything about it is on a larger scale, and a far wider range of angling experiences awaits the novice sea angler. Not alone must he familiarise himself with a strange terminology and a novel array of fish species, he must also become familiar with a completely alien, dynamic, salty environment, the sea.

The sea

To become a truly proficient sea angler one must know something of the sea itself, its changing pattern of movements, its moods and at times its extreme force and power.

The ocean may seem to be a large passive homogeneous water mass but, as on land, the topography of the seabed is complex and its azure blue surface hides from view mountains and valleys, troughs and depressions, great deserts of folded sand and symmetrical rocky promontories which, on occasion, look almost artificial.

As with the land, not all areas of the seabed are equally productive. Marine biologists measure productivity in terms of the abundance of animals present in a given area of ocean. The higher the productivity of food organisms (small fish, snails, crustaceans, worms, etc) the greater the densities of sport fish present. Fish are invariably found where food is most abundant, and not necessarily where the angler finds it easiest to cast.

Depth and productivity

Over 70 per cent of the world's surface area is covered by sea, 80 per cent of which is more than 1.5km deep; more than 50 per cent of the ocean contains depths in excess of 4km. The ocean is at its deepest near the Philippines in the Pacific, where depths of 9.5km and above have been recorded. The Atlantic holds troughs 5-6km deep which rise steeply in places to within a kilometre or less of the surface.

In general, however, the Irish coastline recedes gently into depths of 100fm (200m). Beyond this point it shelves steeply into 1000fm (2000m) and gently falls away into even greater depths. The 100fm (200m) line marks the margin of the continental shelf, which lies off the west coast of Ireland.

Angling is rarely attempted beyond the 50fm (100m) line, indeed the vast majority of sea fish are taken from depths of 30fm (60m) or less.

As one moves into deeper water, pressure and light attenuation become major factors in reducing the abundance of fish stocks. Pressure increases by a factor of 1lb/inch^2/2 feet (0.5kg; 2.5cm^2/60cm), so that at a depth of say 5fm (10m) the pressure will be 15lb/sq. inch (6.5kg/2.5cm^2) greater than at the surface. In the deeper ocean troughs, pressures of 2 to 3 tonnes/2.5cm^2 have been recorded.

Light penetration, which directly regulates the primary productivity of the ocean, is also limited by depth. In the clearest ocean water, only 1 per cent of the light remains at 150m; in average coastal water, at 10m; and in really turbid water at only 1m. As a result, along the 10fm (20m) line, fish live in murky, dull conditions, while those living at 100fm (200m) or more are in a world of perpetual darkness. These depths are not entirely without light, however, for intermittent shafts of biologically generated silver phosphorescence pierce the darkness. The fish and invertebrates that have, surprisingly, adapted so well to life in the deeper ocean troughs — mainly scavengers, living off the dead organisms that rain down from the more productive ocean layers above — have characteristically suffered an almost complete loss of pigment, though many of them possess luminous organs and appendages. These periodically omit an intense phosphorescence, the exact nature of which continues to baffle scientists.

Radiation from the sun warms only a thin surface layer of the ocean. More than 90 per cent of the heat is absorbed in the upper 20m of the clearest ocean waters and in the upper 4m of the average coastal waters. All waters below are warmed by mixing with the surface layers.

Plankton

Basic to life in the ocean are the teeming myriads of tiny animals and plants which inhabit its surface layers. They are known as plankton and may be divided into phytoplankton (the plant component) and zooplankton (floating animal life). The tiny zooplankton feed voraciously on the blooms of phytoplankton until supplies are exhausted, after which they themselves suffer a sharp decline in population numbers. The release of nutrients into the surface of the ocean, particularly following spring or autumnal storms, causes the phytoplankton to bloom once again and the whole cycle is repeated.

The biological pyramid of life in the ocean is dependent on its planktonic base, which is constantly grazed by the smaller fish and, indeed, by some of the more specialised giants of the sea (eg basking sharks, baleen whales). An integral part of this planktonic soup are the eggs and larvae of many ocean fish and invertebrates. To the angler, its greatest practical importance lies in the fact that the diurnal vertical movement of the plankton regulates the depth at which many plankton-feeding fish and their attendant predators reside.

Temperature and salinity

Fish location and, to an extent, abundance are also regulated by both temperature and salinity. Water is, in general, slower than land to absorb heat, but once the ocean temperature has risen, heat is only slowly lost, particularly from its deeper layers. In the shallow areas around our coast, however, heat is gained and lost far more quickly. Fish respond accordingly: for example, cod only venture onto the beaches in late September or early October when autumnal frosts have cooled these marginal areas. Bass, pollack, mullet, ray and plaice will quickly vacate such conditions in favour of the warmer, deeper ocean layers.

Under calm summer conditions the ocean often becomes stratified, with a warm surface layer floating on top of a much cooler, deeper layer. Between the two is an area of rapidly falling temperature, known as the thermocline, which effectively seals in the deeper layer and the all-important nutrients described previously. The sea remains stratified until a storm causes a thorough mixing of layers.

The salinity of the ocean is measured in parts per thousand of salt ($^o/_{oo}$) and is generally in the region of $35^o/_{oo}$. However, in areas where the sea is heavily diluted by large river basins (eg Irish and North Seas), the salinity may drop to $34^o/_{oo}$. Salmonids are most adept at moving from fresh water to the sea without undue hardship. Their unique physiology ensures that they can actively secrete excess salt and retain water when at sea. While most sea fish are solely confined to a marine existence, some estuarine species (eg shad, bass, mullet and flounder) can tolerate brackish or even, in some cases, true fresh water.

Tides

Probably the most remarkable feature of the ocean is its tides and many anglers fish their whole lives without even a basic understanding of how and why tides flow and ebb. The movement and feeding patterns of fish are so intimately dependent on tidal movements that it is worth spending a little time discussing the tides and their periodicity.

Tides are caused by the gravitational forces of the moon and, to a lesser extent, the sun, as they rotate about the earth. Water is actually pulled across the surface of the earth and is concentrated beneath the position of the moon. The moon circles the earth every twenty-eight days, while at the same time the earth rotates on its axis once every twenty-four hours. The combined effect of the sun and moon's gravitational forces and the earth's rotation creates a continuous, sinusoidal,

31

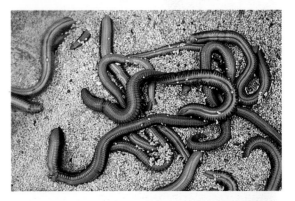

Standard baits for many east coast anglers — lugworm and freshwater roach

Immaculately peeled crab portions

White magic — white ragworm stored in coral sand and sea water

Sea jigs — Hookai mini-baits and mackerel feathers

Returning your fish unharmed to the water is a key ingredient of modern sea angling. This rather perplexed dogfish looks just a little forlorn as he decides whether or not to take the plunge

Well known sea angler Liam Kane, with a good bag of lesser spotted dogfish oceanic tidal wave. In the open sea its vertical component is no greater than 60cm, but as it reaches the continental shelf and the shallower inshore waters its speed is reduced but its height increases as the water is forced to mass near the shore. A distinct horizontal component also comes into play as the water is forced to and fro across the margins of the land, resulting in the large discrepancy in water height which is often noted between high and low water marks.

The tidal wave moves east across the open Atlantic and strikes the west and south-west coasts of Ireland at approximately the same time, causing almost simultaneously high and low tides along these coasts. As the tide makes its way through St George's Channel and up the Irish Sea, the time of high water is correspondingly later.

There are two tides daily, one when the moon is directly overhead and the second when it is on the exact opposite side of the earth. As the moon changes its daily position relative to the earth, the time of high water becomes progressively later, usually by a factor of some fifty minutes. This difference may, however, vary from about thirty minutes on spring tides to seventy-five minutes on neap tides. When both the moon and the sun are in direct alignment they are exerting the greatest gravitational power and as a result we see the greatest rise and fall in the tides, the spring tides. ('Spring' is from the old English 'sprungen' meaning 'to rise'; it has nothing to do with the season.) Neap tides occur when the moon and sun are at right angles to one another and are thus exerting the least gravitational pull. Spring tides occur around the time of each new and each full moon. The equinoxes see the greatest high tides of the year, while the smallest occur at mid-summer and mid-winter.

Around the Irish coast tides generally rise through a vertical distance of 3 to 4.5m, however, where there are constrictions or narrows, the rise may be appreciably greater, from 9 to 12m in places. Tides frequently generate currents and streams which may reach considerable strengths at certain points around the coast. Wind also plays a major part in enhancing or retarding the flow of the tide, depending on its direction and strength.

The North Atlantic Drift

The island of Ireland has a total coastline of 3171km, which may be roughly divided into an Atlantic coastline of 2462km, from Carnsore Point to Fair Head, and an Irish sea coastline of 709km.

We are fortunate in the diversity and abundance of fish species which are present around our coast. Due to the influence of the North Atlantic Drift our shores are occasionally visited by species such as the trigger-fish *(Balistes carolinensis)* and the flying-fish *(Exocoetus volitans)* which are normally confined to the Mediterranean and the tropical Atlantic. We also have resident populations of warm water species such as the bass, which are at the northern limits of their distribution.

The Gulf Stream contains enormous quantities of warm water. It has been calculated that near the American coast it is some 80km wide, 300fm (600m) deep, travels at an average speed of 6.5km/hr and transports fifty million tonnes of water per second. As it crosses the Atlantic, side currents move southwards and by the time it reaches the south-west of Ireland it is only carrying ten million tonnes per second. Here the North Atlantic Drift, as it is now known, divides and sends out branches northwards which eventually reach south-west Iceland, west Norway and the southern Barents Sea. The mild winters which we normally experience in Ireland are largely due to the solar energy trapped in the ocean, some two to three years previously, in the area of the Caribbean known as the Sargasso Sea.

The degree of penetration of these warm waters into the North Atlantic is variable and largely regulated by the direction, strength and persistence of the dominant winds in any given year. In summers when east to north-east winds predominate, the ingress of these warmer currents is retarded and with them their beneficial effects. In contrast, prolonged periods of west or south-west winds greatly enhance the effects of the North Atlantic Drift.

Ireland also marks the southernmost limits for the distribution of cold water species such as the torsk *(Brosme brosme)* which is frequently recorded off our coast but is normally associated with the far North Atlantic.

The true North Atlantic species of fish are confined to an area south of a line linking the continental shelf on which Greenland, Iceland and the Faroe Islands stand, with that of the North Sea and Europe. This line marks the location of a submerged mountain range known as the Wyville Thomson Ridge, which divides the Arctic and Atlantic Oceans. Until its discovery in the 1880s, the apparently anomalous distribution of fish and other animals north and south of the ridge was a cause of great puzzlement and wonder to marine biologists and oceanographers alike.

Because of this convergence of cold and warm water species around the Irish coastline, well over 200 species of marine fish have been recorded from Irish coastal waters and many more remain to be discovered.

Pollution

Despite their immense size and volume, all is not well with the oceans of the world; for they are formed from many individual basins which are largely isolated from neighbouring basins or seas. For example, the Irish Sea functions like a great enclosed lake system. The Irish Sea is a confined area of ocean stretching from St George's Channel in the south to the North Channel and covers a surface area of 45 000 km². It is almost totally enclosed by land and plunges to a maximum depth of over 100fm (200m) in the deeper parts of the North Channel. Its turnover rate (or rate at which

The three species of gurnard: tub, red and grey

Pectorals fully splayed, a 5lb specimen tub gurnard comes to the boat

A brace and a half of sparkling mackerel fresh from the briny

With only the friendly glow of a tilly lamp to keep him company, Willie Roche fishes a Kerry bass beach well into darkness

a given volume of water is replaced) has been calculated at one year! So it is no wonder that emissions from Sellafield (formerly Windscale) and other nuclear installations along the western British coastline have resulted in the Irish sea gaining that most unenviable of titles: 'the most radioactive sea in the world'. Great quantities of raw sewage and chemical waste are also dumped into the ocean without any regard for the disruption which may be caused to the delicate food chains and tenuous planktonic webs of the upper ocean. People must learn that the assimilative capacity of even the greatest ocean is finite and that it is not an insatiable sump for all our waste products.

We are fortunate in Ireland that we are largely surrounded by the Atlantic, one of the greatest oceans in the world, whose as yet unsurfeited cleansing powers keep our shores clean and our bays fresh. However, we must never take such inestimable benefits for granted.

The power of the sea
Whether on a beach, a rocky headland or in a boat, the combined forces of tide, current and wind can produce the most startling and unexpected results. Even on a relatively calm day, a great slow swell may develop which can envelop in its trough a full-sized trawler. A moderate breeze blowing across the unimpeded expanses of the ocean can result in a freak wave which will rise 6m or more above normal along a shear rock mark. Love the sea, enjoy the sea, but at all times respect the sea, for in any two-way conflict you are bound to be the loser.

CHAPTER 3

STOCKS & MANAGEMENT

Unlike his freshwater colleagues, the average sea angler pays little attention to the complex area of sea fisheries management, and who can blame him? For the ocean seems so vast and the threat from even local commercial fishing so immense that he imagines an immovable pack of cards, all firmly stacked against him. Stocks concern him more, particularly the fluctuating abundance of the more common species which he often perceives as being solely regulated by the local commercial fishing effort.

To such anglers the inclusion of a chapter on the management of marine stocks may seem out of place in an angling book. However, I believe that it is vital for modern anglers to consider how best they can influence management decisions relating to key sport species or traditional angling marks. Like so many other areas of angling interest, the key to success lies in a realistic understanding of the magnitude of the problems and a good working knowledge of the principles upon which the various regulatory agencies base their far-reaching decisions.

It might be useful at this juncture to mention some technical terms which I will be using throughout this chapter. *Demersal* fish species are those living on or close to the seabed (cod, ray, plaice, conger, etc). *Pelagic* species are to be found between mid-water and the surface. They generally form large shoals. Amongst the demersal and pelagic groups are both *sedentary* and *migratory* species. While most species of sedentary marine fish may display a limited migratory pattern, when feeding or moving to suitable spawning areas, the population is itself localised to a definite area of the sea or coast. True migratory species undertake great annual journeys of many thousands of miles to distinct, geographically separated, feeding and spawning areas (cod, herring, mackerel).

Research and development

The management of marine recreational fisheries in Ireland has been to date mostly limited to angling surveys and the provision of maps, guides and signposting. Relative to the potential value of the industry, the biological input into research and development has been minuscule. In essence, we have not even begun to take the management of our marine recreational fisheries seriously and tend to regard angling catches as a by-catch of surplus stocks from the expanding commercial fishery.

In contrast, Canada and the USA have begun to realise the true economic value and extent of

Steadying a sleek blue shark for the tailer (Photo courtesy CFB)

A bountiful harvest. Just some of the eighteen species of fish taken in a competition from Killala Bay, Co. Mayo

40

their marine sport fisheries. Economic and biological studies have been commissioned to quantify the resource, and marine enhancement programmes are being introduced covering such areas as the construction of artificial reefs and the control and management of key angling zones, where limited entry and gear restrictions are proposed for both commercial and recreational fishing vessels.

Maintaining adequate spawning stocks

In coming to grips with the management of Irish marine recreational species it is important to grasp the scale of the problem facing such populations. For example, it has recently been calculated that man could theoretically remove 34 million tonnes of fish per annum from the Atlantic alone. It is unimaginable that we could over-exploit such a resource but the annual Atlantic fish harvest currently stands at some 24 million tonnes!

Successful management should guarantee that an adequate surplus of each fish species exists for spawning. The angling component may be taken from this surplus since its overall tonnage is a mere fraction of the total commercial catch. In addition, many shore and boat anglers fish under a strict conservation code which hopefully will ensure the continued survival of many sedentary or localised stocks. However, the pelagic species are often subjected to intense commercial pressure from both home and foreign vessels.

It is the impact of these distant water fisheries on our common pelagic species which is often the most difficult for the average angler to comprehend.

Consider the plight of the common mackerel in Dublin Bay. It has often been stated that stocks of mackerel in the bay have declined significantly over the years. Blame for such a decrease is often laid squarely at the *bunt* of the local Howth or Dún Laoghaire trawlers. How fair and accurate are such accusations?

The Dublin Bay mackerel stock is part of the great western mackerel stock. This migratory stock of fish spawns over a wide area from Biscay to the Porcupine Bank, during the period March to June. As the shoals migrate northwards towards their more northerly feeding ground, they traverse all coasts of Ireland, including Dublin Bay.

The size of this western mackerel stock is truly staggering. It has varied from an estimated 3 million tonnes in 1977 to 1¾ million tonnes in 1986. These vast shoals produced 2×10^{15} eggs in 1977 and an estimated 1×10^{15} eggs in 1986. The total commercial catch in 1986 was estimated at 600 000 tonnes, the Irish component of which was 90 000 tonnes or a staggering 200 million mackerel.

It is obvious from the above that, for whatever reason, the total stock of western mackerel has indeed shown a significant decline over the past decade. It is equally obvious that neither the Howth nor the Dún Laoghaire fleet were solely responsible for its decline.

41

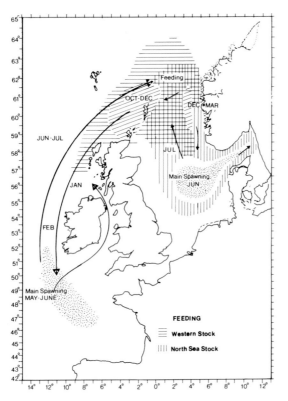

Spawning and feeding migrations of the mackerel

The Irish Sea

Regulating distant water fisheries

Who, then, regulates these distant water fisheries and what is Ireland's role in such decisions? Since the establishment of the EC 200-mile regime in 1977, Brussels has become Ireland's forum for intergovernmental negotiations at the political level. Scientific advice is supplied by ICES (International Council for the Exploration of the Sea), which is headquartered in Copenhagen.

It is an intergovernmental body, set up in 1902, and is totally independent of any other international group or agency. Ireland has been a member in its own right since 1925. Fisheries scientists from member countries recommend a series of Total Allowable Catches (TACs) which are generally adopted and used to set national quotas.

Currently, there are thirteen species to which EC quotas are applied. Some 22 per cent of the TACs set in the EC zone are situated in ICES divisions contiguous to Ireland, and Ireland's share of these is a mere 4.4 per cent. This anomalous position largely arose from the relatively poor state of development of Ireland's deepwater fishing fleet when we first entered the EC.

Whatever about the international complexities of managing migratory stocks, it would seem that the rational exploitation of sedentary stocks, which, theoretically at least, are within our total control, should prove a far easier matter. Currently, our commercial fishermen enjoy exclusive access up to the 19km (12 mile) limit along our northwest and southwest coasts. Elsewhere, France, the United Kingdom and the Netherlands have traditional rights within 9.5-19km (6-12 miles). Spain is excluded to an 80km (50 mile) zone off the coast until 31 December 1995.

Ireland's commercial fishing operations

The size of Ireland's commercial fishing fleet has almost trebled since the mid-seventies and comprises some 2000 registered vessels, 1500 of which are less than 12m in length. A further 1000 vessels, without inboards, are not required to register and the majority of these boats are less than 7m in length. It also comprises a number of so-called super trawlers of between 60 and 90m capable of taking up to 2000 tonnes of fish. To put this in perspective, one three-day trip could provide a meal for 2 million people with a value of over IR£100 000.

It is sad to relate that for many years our sea fisheries have been exploited rather than managed. As one skipper was heard to remark, to make money, one would need to plan two species ahead of BIM (the Irish Sea Fisheries Board). A type of mono-species culture has developed which encourages fishermen to launch wholeheartedly into the exploitation of a single species until returns show a significant drop. At this point the boat is re-equipped, if necessary, to take on a new species until it too begins to decline in abundance.

Such leap-frogging has led to a steep decline in populations of herring and lobster and at present stocks of the long-lived, slow maturing, spur-dogfish are also under threat.

Single species management can also result in unforeseen effects elsewhere in the food chain. For example, cod and *Nephrops* (Dublin Bay prawn) are assessed and managed as independent stocks in the Irish Sea. Research by Irish and British scientists, however, has clearly shown that *Nephrops* is the chief prey of the Irish Sea cod. While the establishment of a flourishing cod stock would

43

be technically possible and economically valuable to achieve, when viewed in isolation, it could only be attained at the direct expense of the *Nephrops* stock, more of which would be eaten by the enhanced cod stock. To make the most of both stocks, managers must evaluate the relative economic benefits from both stocks when viewed as a mutually dependent, continuously interacting resource.

Multi-species management

In general, what is required is a rational multi-species approach to all commercial fisheries whereby each fisherman can take his share of a range of species. An integrated inshore fisheries policy such as that being operated by the Faroese is long overdue. In the Faroese system each fisherman is granted one valuable licence (eg prawn *or* salmon *or* plaice) but is free to fish regulated communal grounds once his main quota has been reached. The quotas are agreed on a yearly basis amongst government scientists and the fishermen's organisations. All catch returns are strictly confidential and are covered by the Statistics Acts which guarantee that fisheries personnel are not permitted to divulge individual catches even to the revenue commissioners!

It is obvious that such an integrated inshore fisheries policy could greatly assist in the regulation and indeed enhancement of marine sport fisheries.

Take, for example, the rational use of wreck marks. Until relatively recently these were primarily the domain of the rod and line angler. However, with the advent of mid-water gill netting, wrecks became a shared resource practically overnight. Commercial interests claim that there is a surplus of fish in or around many wrecks which may be taken without harming the angling potential of these marks. Angling skippers maintain that the larger specimens of such species as ling, pollack, coalfish and conger are quickly removed by the nets and that regular netting over a relatively short period results in a lowering of overall average size. The principal attractions of such wrecks are the range and density of species and high average size present.

In an integrated management context, the local community could decide where the greatest long-term economic gain lay, either in the short-term commercial exploitation of such wrecks or their continued use as self-perpetuating angling marks. I have no doubt that an objective, economically based assessment would come down strongly in favour of the latter option.

Non-quota species

With increasing commercial pressure on a diminishing, or at best stabilised, resource, attention is bound to focus on the non-quota species. Pollack has already been targeted as a possibility and doubtless populations of other sport fish are under consideration. To counter such moves, or at least rationalise them, anglers must press for research into the biology and population dynamics of marine sport fish, for it is impossible to manage an unknown resource rationally. Anglers must also seek economic appraisal of the relative values of our commercial and recreational marine resources.

Long-term management strategies

The long-term management of our inshore waters will necessitate harsh and unpopular decisions. Inshore zoning, long advocated by the Irish Federation of Sea Anglers and involving the allocation of specific sea zones to certain boat sizes, has a definite role to play. The rational exploitation of sedentary species such as sole, brill and turbot, will require that the disruptive influence of the increasingly popular beam trawl or the use of indiscriminate tangle nets is regulated and curtailed. Broadly speaking, the objective of strategic planning should be to adapt the size, composition and activity of the fishing fleets to the resources in the area.

Volunteer guardians

Pollution of bays, estuaries and inlets is also an increasing problem and sea anglers must take even more seriously their role as volunteer guardians of such juvenile habitats. Within these areas the management and protection of bait sources, principally beds of lugworm *(Arenicola)* and ragworm *(Nereis)*, are of vital immediate concern. Such problems mostly arise near centres of high population such as cities and large towns.

I hope this chapter has heightened anglers' awareness regarding the possible long-term problems threatening their sport and encouraged them to campaign for the rational management and conservation of both sedentary and migratory stocks. Anglers and commercial interests must learn to coexist, for the long-term rational exploitation of the sea's bounty is in the interest of all.

CHAPTER 4

ANGLING LOCATIONS & METHODS

Sea angling — a rewarding experience

The sea is a rich and varied environment, containing as it does an infinite variety of animal forms and shapes. No matter how specialised your tackle and techniques, it will constantly surprise you; a large pollack or bass on shark tackle or a tope from the beach or rocks, dabs on cod rigs and cod on dab or flounder rigs, all are common occurrences. Even novice shore anglers are guaranteed eventual success, but this bountiful harvest has resulted in an impression that sea angling is simple, crude, a mug's game, involving little or no planning or skill. It is denigrated by those who have little or no knowledge of it, but revered by those fortunate enough to have sampled its delights. Successful and pleasant sea angling is dependent on suitable balanced tackle and a careful choice of both quarry and location. There is little pleasure in hauling up strings of ½lb (230g) whiting on a light boat rod from 8 to 10fm (16-20m) but conversely, the first long searing run of a powerful tope on similar tackle is an exciting and memorable event.

Thankfully, many sea anglers now fish under strict conservation principles and gone are the days when every fish taken was killed. The sight of many tonnes of dead and decaying fish lying on the piers of Westport, Valentia or Ballycotton, following a large international competition, did little to further the perception of sea angling as a sport. Gone also are the days when the discarded remains of dogfish, tope and shark littered the seabed at the base of piers and jetties. Except in the case of small localised or sedentary stocks (monkfish populations in Clew Bay), the actual quantities of fish taken were probably small relative to the total stocks present but their wasteful slaughter made a nonsense of any argument put forward in favour of the rational management and exploitation of marine resources.

Local knowledge

Although fish may come your way at almost every stage of the tide, the consistently successful angler will be found at the right time, in the right place, at the right stage of the tide. Each beach has its own rhythm and pattern, and local knowledge is an invaluable asset along a strange shoreline. Two beaches only hundreds of yards apart may display completely different angling patterns.

To amass a fund of sea angling knowledge, you are well advised to keep an accurate diary of tides, weather, fishing locations, baits used and catches taken. Over time you will find a definite pattern emerging, especially for those beaches or marks which you fish most consistently. A diary will pay handsome dividends.

When boat fishing, a knowledge of the tides and currents will not alone improve your success rate but will also guarantee a safe and swift journey to and from the fishing grounds. To move out with the ebb and home with the flood may result in an extra hour or more fishing time.

Let us now review the different types of angling locations and the tackle and bait required for consistent success.

Shore fishing

The term 'shore' covers all non-boat angling, whether it is carried out from a beach, a rocky plateau, a pier or a breakwater.

Shingle/cobble beaches

The shingle or cobble beach is normally a steep shelving beach of rough gravel and stone, frequently subjected to strong wave action in the form of storms or strong currents. Storm beaches display strong lateral tidal movements and these may carry heavy loads of loose weed, even under relatively calm conditions. Although the tidal zone of such areas is generally polished clean, they shelve quickly into deep water, and good populations of sandeels and other small fish may be present. Storm beaches are frequented by cod and small coalfish in autumn and winter, and by bass, flatfish and the occasional tope in summer. Although primarily confined to the coast of the Irish Sea, small cobble beaches are also to be found throughout the south and western coastal areas.

Surf beaches

Surf beaches are more consolidated than storm beaches and contain finer gravels and sand. They are generally westward facing and occur along all coasts except the east and north eastern coasts. Surf beaches are quite shallow at low water and might appear to be relatively barren. However, when the great Atlantic rollers come cascading in from the west, the turbulent water tables between the breakers carry a surprising array of food organisms, from shrimp to crabs and small fish. These beaches normally carry two to five breakers, depending on the wind's strength and duration. Despite their apparent turbulence, there are no lateral movements present along such beaches and floating weed is far less of a problem. However, when weed does gather in appreciable quantities it may take several weeks to disperse. Surf beaches are well known for bass, but they also produce flounder, dabs, ray and in places tope. Sea trout may also be present, especially along the more northerly beaches of Sligo and Donegal.

Mud flats

Gently sloping mud flats are extremely rich in marine life and in season harbour hordes of juvenile fish larvae and fry. Their distinctive corrugated, rippled surface is home to a whole range of important bait animals, such as lugworm, white ragworm, razorfish and cockles. They can be dangerous places to fish, for they are drained by an interwoven complex of channels or streams. When fishing on the outer edge of a mud flat the preoccupied angler could be easily marooned by the rapid pincer movement of two flooding channels. Mud flats are flounder country *par excellence* and these plucky fighters are principally found in the channels and streams. Bass, mullet and the occasional ray may also be present.

Piers and jetties

Piers and jetties come in all shapes and sizes. They may be located either on deep, fast-flowing estuaries or alongside deepwater marks on the open coast. If you can ignore the trappings of technological progress that generally surround you in such places, they can be truly exciting venues to fish. They offer the shore angler the opportunity to encounter really large deepwater species from the shore. Ray, skate, tope, monkfish, ling, large cod have all been taken from such marks. Remember that those situated on large estuaries (eg Foynes, County Limerick) may be influenced by the degree of dilution present. Under drought conditions true saltwater fish may penetrate far into the estuary, but as the freshwater influence increases, species such as ray and skate are forced to migrate towards more saline conditions. Piers and jetties offer the opportunity to catch a wide range of different species. A total of six to eight is not uncommon for a five- to six-hour session.

Rocks

Rock fishing is a speciality and should only be attempted by the novice in the company of experienced companions. The rewards can be exciting but the risks are at times great. Some marks involve climbs of 15 to 30m down broken rockfaces. The quarry is normally wrasse, pollack, conger, tope or ling. The attraction is the deep water close by and the great surge and motion of the tide which exaggerates every movement of a hooked fish. Landing your prize can be a problem and both a dropnet and a good stout gaff are standard equipment. **Freak waves may prove fatal if the angler is not alert and ever vigilant. Rock fishing should never be attempted on your own, for even a minor fall could quickly develop into a major tragedy.**

Shore tackle

Shore tackle is obviously as varied as the habitats described above. Thankfully, however, it may be broken down into three major categories and an optional fourth type(s):

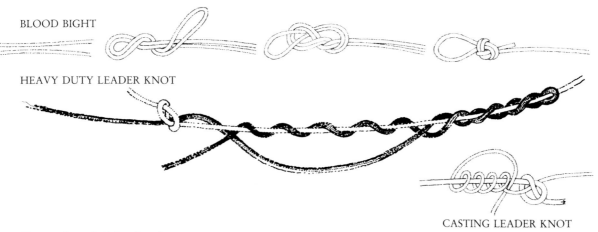

BLOOD BIGHT

HEAVY DUTY LEADER KNOT

CASTING LEADER KNOT

Storm beach/pier/rocks

Rugged gear is required to make the most of bottom fishing these venues. The tackle must also be capable of casting moderate distances and of providing a reasonable level of sensitivity. It may be called on to handle anything from a 1½lb (0.5kg) codling to a 30lb+ (13.5kg+) conger. The ideal tackle is an 11-13ft (3.5-4m) thick-walled fibreglass beachcaster capable of handling a 4-8oz (113-230g) lead and of casting distances of 100 to 120m when required. Since the introduction of carbon fibre in 1975 much debate has centred around its role in sea angling equipment. The original pure carbon beach rods had a tendency to snap under strain but more recently a carbon/fibreglass mix seems, largely, to have overcome this problem. The ideal companion for such a rod is one of the modern multipliers, which is itself filled with 300m of 15-20lb (6.5-9kg) monofilament.

Some anglers prefer the large fixed-spool reels and there is no doubt that they can function quite effectively. However, they are mounted away from the rod itself and can be very difficult to crank when heavy quantities of drifting weed are about. The multiplier is mounted facing the angler and so the full power of the rod is available for both striking and retrieving line. The multiplier also possesses higher gear ratios and the tackle may be retrieved more quickly and with less effort. The ratchet on the multiplier, when the reel is set on free spool, may act as an excellent bite indicator.

Terminal rigs are connected to the main line via a shock leader. This is a 10 to 12m length of strong, 40-60lb (18-27kg) monofilament which is joined directly to the main line by means of a special blood-knot. When the angler is casting a heavy lead, great force is exerted on the main line as it is punched out seawards. The shock leader is designed to take the brunt of the force and to avoid line breakages. Even a two ounce (56g) lead is a potentially lethal projectile as it is forced out to sea at speeds of 160 kmph or more. How much more lethal is a 4-6oz (113-170g) grip lead!

Always exercise the utmost care when casting, particularly in the dark or where there are children or onlookers about. It is amazing the varied directions which a lead, severed from the main line, can take. I have seen snapped leads flying horizontally along the beach, to land in the water only yards away from neighbouring anglers.

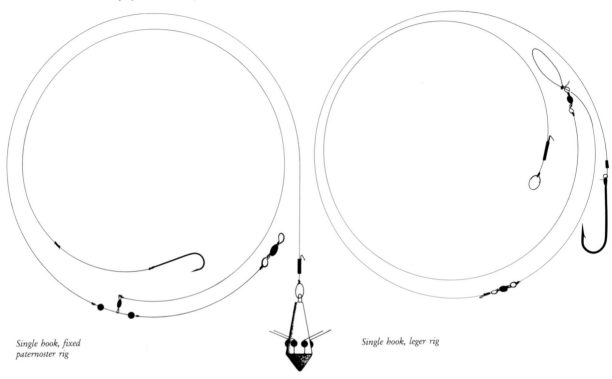

Single hook, fixed paternoster rig

Single hook, leger rig

Terminal rigs fall into two basic sub-categories, fixed paternoster and running leger, and these may carry from one to three droppers or snoods. Snoods are generally formed from blood-loops, link swivels or patent semi-stiff or stiff booms; fashioned from pliable plastic, rigid plastic or even wire. I have found the simple blood-loop snood to be quite adequate although the pliable plastic snood, when used in conjunction with a bait clip, ensures that the rig plus bait is more streamlined and greater distances may be achieved. I normally limit myself to one or at most two hooks. A single hook rig is more adaptable and may be fished with either a short or long snood designed for bottom feeders or a long flowing trace which suspends the bait just off the bottom in the tide.

The fixed paternoster is normally used under rough or difficult conditions, while the running leger is ideal for calmer weather.

I should make mention of bait clips which are shown on some of the diagrams. These are an ingenious invention designed to reduce air resistance by keeping the bait attached to the line until the weight touches the water. On impact, the trace folds, releasing the hook from the bait clip. When casting it is the pressure of the lead which keeps the hook in place. Bait clips may be manufactured using paper clips and the plastic coating from electric wire. Patent plastic or metal clips may also be purchased.

Surf beaches/estuaries/sandy bays

To tackle such locations the angler should, ideally, be equipped with a light 10-11ft (3-3.5m) light-walled beachcaster capable of handling a 2 to 4 oz (56-113g) lead. The line should consist of 150 to 200m of 12-15lb (5.5-6.5kg) monofilament and a 10m shock leader of 20-25lb (9-11kg) breaking strain. The reel should be capable of carrying some 250m of 12-15lb (5.5-6.5kg) monofilament — a modern multiplier reel is best.

Such tackle is normally used by the bass angler but may also be called upon to land flounder, ray and even the occasional tope, although the first searing run of a medium to large tope might well outstrip the line capacity available. If there is a good chance of tope, my advice would be to revert to the heavier beach tackle described previously.

Again, there are two basic rigs, the fixed and the running leger. One or two hooks may be used and there are certainly initial advantages to using a two-hook trace in that a selection of baits may be tried over a relatively short period of time. Many experienced anglers stick to a simple fixed paternoster even under relatively calm conditions.

Before leaving beachcasters, I should say a word or two about casting, for in practically no other area of our sport is casting technique so important. From both the safety point of view and from the point of view of adaptability, casting is crucial to success. It cannot be adequately covered within the context of a general book such as the present one and I would therefore advise the novice sea angler to seek some expert tuition before venturing out on a beach with a strong beachcaster and 6oz (170g) of potentially lethal lead.

Light ground fishing/spinning

A strong 9-11ft (2.5-3.5m) salmon spinning rod can adequately deal with this form of bottom fishing. No shock leader is required and plain Arlesey bombs of 1-2oz (28-56g) are normally used in conjunction with a fixed-spool reel capable of holding 150m of 10-12lb (4.5-5.5kg) nylon. To the main line is attached a simple one- or two-hook fixed paternoster or running leger. This tackle will primarily take flounder and estuarine bass but may also be used from a boat for light ray fishing in sheltered estuaries or bays. The rod may also be used when spinning for such species as pollack, coalfish, mackerel, bass or shad. However, in more sheltered situations a lighter 8-10ft (2.5-3m) rod and 8lb (3.5kg) main line would be more suitable and more fun to use.

Shore spinning normally takes place from piers, jetties or rocky platforms which shelve off steeply into deep water. Relatively little spinning is carried out from strands or beaches. This is a great pity for spinning from such locations can prove quite productive and may produce surprisingly good catches of mackerel, bass, coalfish and sea trout.

Float rod/fly rod

These two rods are largely luxury or specialist items since the species taken by float fishing or on the fly may be taken by methods described previously. However, both rods are sensitive and light and guarantee the angler more direct contact with some of the sea's most sporting species.

A standard 11-13ft (3.5-4m) fibreglass or carbon float rod and a fixed-spool reel armed with 100 to 150m of 8-10lb (3.5-4.5kg) main line will enable the angler to float fish for such species as pollack, coalfish, mackerel, bass and mullet. A simple waggler float set for either a fixed distance or used as a sliding float completes the rig.

Fly fishing in the sea is little practised in Europe but has been extensively used in North America to take such hard fighting species as tarpon and bone fish. Fly fishing in Irish waters can produce sea trout, bass, mackerel, shad, pollack and coalfish. The technique is generally used in estuaries, bays and inlets but can take surface feeding predatory fish on the open sea. The tackle normally consists of a 9-10ft (2.5-3m) strong, full action reservoir rod, a size 8 to 10 forward tapered sink-tip or slow-sinking line and 100m of strong backing. An 8-10ft (2.5-3m), 8-10lb (3.5-4.5kg) cast is normally used and the flies are attractor lures, suggestive of small fish or fry.

Inshore fishing

Using dinghies

The use of mobile, 12-16ft (3.5-5m) boats for inshore sea fishing is growing in popularity. These small craft are manoeuvrable and are easily launched by two anglers. They are normally carried about on a boat trailer and are launched from a convenient beach or slipway along a likely looking shoreline. The use of dinghies has opened up a wide range of possibilities for inshore angling and has resulted in the discovery of productive inshore marks which were previously ignored by the larger boats or unattainable by the shore angler. These boats rarely fish in water deeper than 8fm (16m), largely capitalising on marks within 500m to 5km of the shoreline.

Standard equipment

One to three anglers may fish in a dinghy and it is essential that extra care be given to safety precautions. Standard equipment should include: flares, tool kit, spare spark plugs, shearpins, all stored in a waterproof container. A compass should always be carried in case of fog and an adequate anchor is most important. The anchor rope or warp should be about 20fm (40m) in length. Well-maintained oars and rowlocks are an essential prerequisite in case of engine failure. The boat should be equipped with a strong plastic bailing can and a suitable fish box in which to store the catch. All of the anglers should be equipped with life jackets.

Boat rods

A choice of tackle is available to the dinghy angler. Many simply use their beach equipment but long rods are a definite disadvantage in the rather cramped conditions of a small dinghy. A short 6ft (2m) light boat rod and multiplier reel have now become almost standard tackle.

Boat rods generally come in varying lengths from 6 to 8ft (2–2.5m). They are single-piece rods with a detachable butt into which the single length of glass fibre fits snugly and a locking ring screws into position to secure the parts of the rod. To reduce line friction, good quality boat rods are fitted, both top and bottom, with roller rings.

Boat rods are classified according to their test curve (the weight needed to pull the tip of the rod through 90°) and it is normal to use a line approximately five times heavier than the test curve weight. Thus a line of 10lb (4.5kg) would be used on a rod with a 2lb (1kg) test curve and a 20lb (9kg) line on a rod with a 4lb (2kg) test curve.

For dinghy fishing, a 12–20lb (5.5–9kg) class rod would be used in conjunction with a large shore multiplier capable of holding 200 to 300m of 15–25lb (6.5–11kg) main line. When boat fishing, the drag or tension system used can be quite important and while the standard star drag system is fine for most situations, a more accessible lever drag system is a great advantage when you encounter a strong fast-moving fish such as a tope or a large smooth hound. If you are likely to encounter a really large fish (eg monkfish, conger), the drum of the multiplier should be made of metal and not plastic. When under extreme tension, monofilament displays an amazing degree of stretch. If wound onto the drum in a taut state, it later seeks to revert to its original shape, contracts and ruptures or distorts the plastic drum.

53

Terminal rigs

Terminal rigs for boat fishing are basically variations on those listed earlier for use from the shore and include both fixed paternoster and running leger rigs. One interesting addition is the sliding boom. This clever device is normally armed with a pyramid lead. This digs into the bottom, much like a plough shear but allows the main line to run freely through the apertures on top of the boom. Fixed boom paternoster rigs are often used when bottom fishing from boats. They may be lowered over the side without any of the disadvantages mentioned earlier when using fixed booms from the shore.

In recent years, a technique called 'up-tide' fishing has become very popular amongst dinghy fishermen. This involves casting the terminal tackle as far up tide as possible from an anchored boat. Grip leads are used to prevent the tackle being pulled back by the tide towards the boat. The line is tightened hard into the lead until the tip of the rod takes a slight curve. When the fish takes the bait the lead is released, the rod tip straightens and the fish has generally hooked himself by the drag of the spiked lead. In such situations there is a definite advantage in using a slightly longer (8ft; 2.5m) rod.

A partial leger, incorporating a clements boom

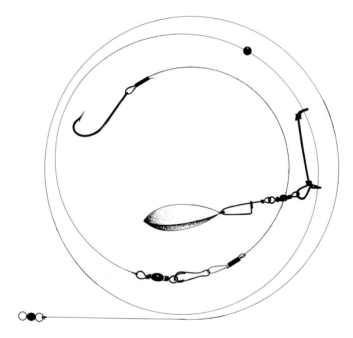

Spinning

In addition to legering on the bottom, the dinghy angler may also spin, drift-line, troll or drift with the tide. Spinning is normally done with a salmon-type reel similar to that described for shore fishing. The choice of baits is almost limitless but amongst the firm Irish favourites are rubber eels, wagtails, german sprats, mackerel feathers, Toby's and Tobis lures. The trace consists of a kidney or wye-lead, and a 3–4ft (1m) trace attached to the plain or link swivel on the desired lure. If preferred, a plastic anti-kink may also be added.

Drift-lining

Drift-lining is designed to take full advantage of a strong tide or current. It is normally used from an anchored boat; the bait or lure is lowered into the water and line is paid out until it is fishing at the desired depth and distance from the angler. Sufficient weight is used to ensure that the bait is located at the required depth for the species being sought. Movement is imparted to the bait by the action of the tide and the intermittent movement of the rod tip by the angler. Both natural baits (slips of mackerel or sandeels) and artificials may be used and the strength of the tackle should match the size of the intended quarry.

Trolling

Trolling is a popular method of fishing for fast-moving predatory fish such as pollack, bass, mackerel and sea trout. Various species of fish are to be found at varying depths during the day. For example, to fish for pollack you must troll slow and deep, while for bass, mackerel or sea trout you must troll closer to the surface and at a faster speed. Downriggers (such as the tidebeater described previously, see page 227) are becoming increasingly popular with dinghy anglers for they allow them to fish at a whole range of predetermined depths with lighter, more responsive tackle. When fishing a shoal, remember not to drive directly through it but rather skirt the shoal, picking up fish as you go. When fishing a strong tideway, move forward and backwards across the tide rather than either directly with or against the current. Your bait will cover a great deal more fish when criss-crossing the current.

Drifting

Drifting, to be really effective, should be carried out at a slow, steady pace. For this reason, light fibreglass dinghies are not the ideal craft from which to attempt this method of fishing. However, by the judicious use of a drogue or light anchor, the speed of the drift may be significantly reduced. Standard boat fishing tackle is used and the terminal rig may be either a fixed paternoster or a running leger. To leger, use a long flowing trace or a string of baited mackerel feathers. The rig is lowered until the lead touches the bottom and at this point some 6-8ft (2-2.5m) is wound back onto the reel. A drifting boat will almost invariably encounter rough ground and for this reason the weight should be attached to the trace by 8-12in (20-30cm) of weaker nylon — so-called 'rotten bottom'. If the sinker snags, the remainder of the trace can be easily salvaged and a new lead attached. Since the boat is constantly moving, strike all bites and be alert for depth changes which will require that the bait be either raised clear of an underwater peak or lowered to find the bed of a deeper trough.

Deep sea fishing

A specialist sport

Deep sea angling is generally carried out from half-deckers, trawlers or angling boats, at depths of 10 to 30fm (20-60m) or more. It is a specialist sport requiring strong, reliable, well-maintained tackle, a good knowledge of the most productive grounds and the ability to locate and anchor just off key marks. Unlike most other branches of angling practised in Ireland, tackle is normally included in the charter price. One disadvantage is that, at times, one finds a range of skills on board, from the complete novice to the species specialist. A good skipper will, however, attempt to match the skills of his anglers and to ensure that grounds are fished which will satisfy their particular requirements. A novice may enjoy two or three hours of 'pollack bashing' while the specialist may well prefer two hours of patient waiting and the chance of a really large conger or ling.

Boat rods and reels

Deep sea angling normally involves the use of a 6-7ft (2m) fibreglass, 30-50lb (13.5-22.5kg) class boat rod. Where the quarry are really large (eg skate, blue shark, porbeagle shark), an 80-100lb (36-45kg) class rod may be used. Good quality fittings are essential for the combination of heavy weights (up to 2lb; 1kg) of lead, strong currents or tides, and a writhing 100lb+ fish tests every centimetre of the tackle to its limit. Good quality boat rods are fitted with roller rings, top and bottom, which considerably lessen the friction when hauling heavy weights from great depths. There should be no chance of the rod rotating within the butt and most rods contain a V-notch which slips over a bar inside the butt, thus preventing rotation. Deep sea rods are also fished in combination with a stiff leather butt rest. This is strapped around the waist of the angler and the base of the rod fits snugly into the rest, which hangs down towards the base of the stomach. It is of great assistance when levering large fish off the bottom and even the most macho of anglers soon learn that a bruised stomach or crotch is a dear price to pay for landing a large fish unaided.

As mentioned previously, deep sea reels should have a large capacity (300m of 60lb; 27kg) and the spool should be made from metal and not plastic. Monofilament is fine in strengths up to 30lb (13.5kg) but when fishing for heavier fish you are well advised to use Dacron or Terylene braided nylon. It does not stretch to the same degree as monofilament and is thinner for the equivalent breaking strain. Pre-stretched monofilament was recently introduced onto the market and appears to have overcome many of the problems attached to the use of standard monofilament. On large multipliers a lever drag system is much preferable to the traditional star drag. It is easier to manoeuvre and can achieve a much finer degree of adjustment.

Rigs

Terminal rigs for deep sea fishing are legion but normally include both variations on the fixed paternoster and the running leger systems. Multi-hook rigs are used when fishing a fixed lead for the smaller bottom-feeding fish, particularly if you want to test a range of baits. However, where large fish are the quarry, I would prefer a single hook attached to a clements boom type running leger.

Many of the larger predatory fish caught in deep water have sharp shearing teeth which will easily cut through soft monofilament or braided nylon traces. For this reason it is standard practice to include a length of wire in the trace. There are two schools of thought on this matter: one belief is that 6 to 12in (15–30cm) of 300lb (136kg) strain multi-strand wire (Alasticum) attached to 6 to 8ft (2–2.5m) of 80lb (36kg) nylon is the ideal rig; while the other opinion is that 1m of 100lb (45kg) strain wire and a proportionately shorter heavy nylon trace is preferable. The long trace is essential for rough-skinned species such as the shark and ray whose hide is coated with sharp, small, teeth-like projections. If wrapped around the trace, such fish can easily flitter lighter nylon to shreds.

Wire is secured by means of small wire tubes known as ferrules or sleeves. The wire is passed through the eye of the hook twice and folded back into the slieve before it is securely crimped, firmly and evenly, along the length of the joining. A similar system is used to form a loop at the swivel end of the trace. A link swivel is normally incorporated in the loop and hook lengths may then be readily clipped on and off as required. You are well advised to make up a range of traces before going on board the boat, for there is nothing more agonising than wasting valuable fishing time fiddling about with ferrules, wire and pliers on the deck of a heaving, tossing boat.

Guarding against corrosion

Corrosion is a major problem, which constantly threatens the sea angler's tackle. It is insidious by nature and will quietly chew away at the tiniest portion of exposed metal. It is vital to be ever vigilant against the dangers of corrosion for not alone will it cost you dearly in tackle replacement and but it may also result in the loss of some exceptionally large fish.

Guarding against corrosion is not easy, but if you keep your reels well oiled and greased and wash them thoroughly in fresh water after each trip, you should largely avoid the problem. It is best to immerse the reels fully in water rather than simply passing them under a running tap. After removing them from their bath, shake off the excess water and wind the handle several times to release any water which has lodged internally. Leave the reels to drain in a bucket or basin overnight; wipe dry the following morning and re-oil or grease as necessary.

Rods should also be washed down in fresh water after use. Be particularly careful with the metal reel seat: I recently broke the mount off my beach multiplier by neglecting to clean out some sand grains which had lodged inside the reel sleeve. As a consequence, the reel mount was insecure and shattered as it rocked about when I was casting.

Keep all your hooks and baits in secure plastic containers. Watch out for spray, droplets of which may lodge in the lid or base of an open box. It is good practice to check all boxes for signs of damp when you return from a sea angling trip. Finally, remember to wash all ancillary equipment such as knives, pliers, forceps, etc.

Hooks and swivels

Although hooks represent the most important part of the sea angler's armoury, it is amazing how many anglers take the choice of size and design of hook for granted. Sea angling may require hooks from sizes 8 to 8/0 or even 10/0, depending on the species sought, but in general the shore angler uses sizes 1/0 to 5/0 and the boat angler (deep sea) 5/0 to 8/0. The design of the hook is equally important. I would recommend either forged stainless steel hooks or those plated in either cadmium or tin. I have also found chemically sharpened hooks to be excellent, but they have one disadvantage: their needle-sharp points require constant re-sharpening when fishing over rough ground. Bronzed hooks are popular amongst sea anglers but they are easily corroded and if such decay goes unnoticed they may snap at the bend. Smaller hooks, sizes 2 to 8, are useful for estuarine fishing, especially for mullet and flounder. To sharpen your hooks, always carry a small light file.

One word of warning regarding hooks with strongly incurved points: they are excellent hooks to hold a fish once the barb has penetrated the fish's mouth but in my experience they are poor at hooking fish. Such hooks frequently carry small projections along the shank, designed to hold the bait firmly in place. These look well but are largely unnecessary.

On occasions, the sea angler will also need to use a whole series of split links, swivels, link swivels, snap links, etc. As in the case of hooks, always purchase the best quality available, for these items form a vital link between the trace and the angler. Make sure that they are corrosion proof, particularly swivels which should rotate freely. I have some reservations regarding snap links and

Trench digging for lugworm on Sandymount Strand

link swivels and prefer, especially when long casting is required, to use a good quality split link, which cannot possibly prise open.

Bait

Collecting and choosing bait

Good quality, fresh bait is basic to a successful day's sea angling. To obtain bait, the angler may choose to dig or net it, or it may be purchased from a fish shop or tackle dealer. Collecting your own bait has several advantages: it ensures that the bait is truly fresh, you are guaranteed a good supply and variety of baits, and it is simply more fun. For me, bait digging is the starter, while catching fish is the main course: it whets the appetite, fires the imagination and leaves you with that very special, lingering smell and taste of the sea.

The ocean is a rich and diverse habitat and almost every creature is a potential source of bait for the angler. Some, however, have proven themselves to fish consistently well over the years and it is these which we will concentrate on. Others may still remain to be discovered and if you find yourself short of bait, experiment, for limpets, periwinkles, cockles, and even uneaten sandwiches have all taken fish!

Lugworm (Arenicola marina)

One of the most commonly used baits in Ireland, the lugworm, may be found in firm, wet sand throughout the middle shoreline. It lives about 8 to 12m (20-30cm) below the surface in a U-shaped burrow. As it moves down into the sand it consumes sand grains, from which it absorbs particles of plant material and bacteria. The sand is then expelled up towards the surface where it forms the distinctive casts so characteristic of lugworm beds. The burrow is delineated by the casts at one end and a small hole or depression at the other end.

Lugworm may be either dug individually or, where they are plentiful, by trench digging. I prefer to use a fork rather than a spade when digging bait as I find that it results in less broken worms. When digging individual lug, the first forkful is taken from the depression end of the burrow, a second forkful is taken from the cast end and the third is angled in from the side, slightly off centre. This final forkful should contain the worm. On strands with a large exposed area of sand and also during the colder winter months, lugworm may dig deeply into the sand and become difficult to locate. Trench digging involves the excavation of a face some 2 to 3m long which is then dug in sequence from side to side. Sometimes a false face may be required to drain the surface water from the area of the strand where the lugworm are located. Simply dig a trench and allow the surface water to discharge into it. Move back a metre or so and commence on a second trench.

Lugworm are best stored on flat, dry sheets of newspaper. By far the most suitable containers for storage are a series of shallow wooden bakers' trays. Two to three layers of worms can be placed on top of one another in each tray, provided the layers are not densely packed.

Lugworm are best mounted on the hook by means of the tail end or sand sac; the juicy head and entrails are thus located near the hook end. As well as the larger 6 to 8m (15–20cm) reddish or brownish black lugworm, a smaller lugworm may be found in the softer mud of estuaries. This is known as a blower lug and is also a good bait, but in really soft, gooey areas its collection may be problematical.

Ragworm (*Nereis* spp.)
The common bronze ragworm is an excellent all-round bait and is to be found in banks along the middle and lower shore. It is more localised in its distribution than the lugworm and the banks are often found just above the low tide mark. Ragworm are normally some 3 to 8in (7.5–20cm) long and have a whole series of centipede-type legs running along both flanks. They are carnivorous creatures and possess strong, sharp black pincers which can give the unwary collector a painful nip. However, if you hold the ragworm firmly behind the head, it will be unable to manoeuvre its head back to bite you.

There are also three other types of ragworm which the shore angler will encounter. These are the king ragworm (which may grow up to an incredible 18in; 46cm), the small red ragworm and the white ragworm or herringbone. The latter is one of my favourite baits and may also be found in appreciable numbers amongst the lugworm beds.

Ragworm are very hardy and can be held for quite an appreciable time if handled carefully. Spread the worms out, thinly, amongst a layer of damp seaweed and store in an absorbent cloth sack. You may also layer ragworm in a similar fashion to lugworm, but be sure to leave plenty of breathing space between the worms. Store the worms in a cool place, remove the dead individuals each morning and they will last for well over a week.

Ragworm is mounted on the hook head first and if using extra large rag, do not be afraid to break the worm into two or three separate segments. Beware, however, for such broken portions can quickly decompose, particularly in warm summer weather; discard all unused segments as soon as they stop wiggling.

Crabs
A great variety of crabs inhabit the rocky margins of our coastline but as far as the sea angler is concerned, the three most important bait species are shore crab (*Carcinus maenas*), the velvet swimming crab *(Macropipus puber)* and the edible crab *(Cancer pagurus)*. All crabs are encased in

a rigid unyielding shell which must first be cast if they are to grow. It is when the shell is about to be cast ('peeler' stage) or has just been discarded ('softie' stage) that crabs are at their most vulnerable to predators. At this time they are secreting specialised hormones which bring about these changes and fish find the taste of such hormones irresistible.

Soft crabs are easy to detect and unlike the aggressive hardback are frequently found cowering under weeds or stones in or adjacent to small rock pools. Press your finger against its back and you will sense the supple leathery texture of the skin. When you find two crabs moving along piggy-back style, you can be sure that the passenger is a soft female.

Peelers are a little more difficult to detect but again they have a great tendency to stay well under cover. They are normally duller in colour than the hard-back crab but the only definitive method of identifying a peeler is to break off one of its legs near a joint and if the shell comes away clean, revealing a complete limb coated in a soft, light, hairy skin, then you have indeed located a peeler. If the shell comes away with pieces of muscle and flesh adhering to it, then it is a hard-back.

Crabs can be used whole or in portions. In general, the smaller crabs are used whole while large specimens are divided to make two or three baits. Soft crabs may be mounted directly onto a hook but peelers must have all of the old shell or carapace removed from the back, front and legs. Peeler crabs may be stored for several days in a wooden box lined with damp seaweed. A lid is an essential item to prevent escape. Keep the weed moist by dampening it with salt water every two days or so. The new shell oxidises and hardens quickly on soft crabs and there is little point in storing them for longer than a day, or at most two days.

To attach a crab, pass the hook through the base of the leg and out through the crab's back. To secure the crab you may either attach two or three legs to the trace by means of elasticated thread or alternatively the thread may be wrapped around the body, securing the shank of the hook.

Sandeels (*Hyperoplus* Sp. and *Ammodytes* Sp.)
An increasingly popular bait amongst anglers in Ireland, good quality frozen sandeels are now readily available from many of the larger tackle dealers in the cities and larger towns. Sandeel is an item which appears regularly in the stomachs of many of the more popular sea fish, particularly bass, sea trout, pollack and turbot. There are two different species of sandeel — the greater sandeel *(Hyperoplus lanceolatus)* which grows to 12in (30cm) or more and the lesser sandeel *(Ammodytes tobianus)* which grows to no more than 5 or 6in (13–15cm). It is a denizen of the lower shore and is found in loose, coarse sand, just above or immediately below the low tide mark. It is either a feast or famine when collecting sandeel.

When collecting sandeels, a fork or a sickle with V-shaped notches cut along its length is drawn through the sand and the buried sandeels are thrown up on the surface in its wake. In the south of England, where sandeels are particularly abundant, a special tool known as a 'vingler' is used. Its flat, blunt blade has a hooked end in which the sandeels are trapped. Sandeels are amazingly agile and when collecting them, a young, supple assistant is a great advantage.

Sandeels can be used either alive or dead. Live sandeels are mounted by passing a single hook through the upper and out the lower lip. Alternatively, the hook may be passed through the mouth and out the gill. It is attached by slipping the hook through the skin along its flank.

Sandeels are delicate creatures and if you wish to cast any appreciable distance, freshly killed sandeels are a much more reliable proposition. There are a number of rigs which you may use: a single hook is passed through the two lips and a trailing treble hook inserted along the flank, the nylon between single and treble is then secured to the sandeel's body by means of elastic thread; alternatively, a large single may be passed through its mouth and out behind the gill cover. It is then inserted in the flank and again secured by means of elasticated thread.

Prawns and shellfish

Prawns, mussels, cockles, razorfish, clams and limpets are all useful baits and are generally easy to come by.

Prawns can be bought fresh off many small commercial fishing boats and are an excellent bait. The two most common species are those favoured by the salmon angler: the common prawn *(Leander serratus)*, usually 1 to 4in (2.5-10cm) in length and the dwarf prawn *(Leander squilla)* which averages about 2in (5cm) in length. To fish the prawn, insert a straightening pin through the creature from tail to head — a bent paper-clip makes a fine pin — and insert a single or treble hook, sizes 1 to 4, into the ventral surface. Bind the nylon to the shrimp's body using elastic thread.

Mussels are a fine all-round bait and can easily be gathered where mussel beds are present. To open a mussel, place it in the palm of your hand with the valve-opening facing towards you. Insert a sharp thin blade between the valves about half way along its length and prise open the shell. Scour out the mussel by running the blade close to the upper margin of the shell. Mussels are a soft bait and best used from a boat. However, salted mussel can be cast considerable distances. To gain maximum hold, always insert the hook through the tough 'foot' of the mussel.

Razorfish inhabit the lower shore and like the lugworm, burrow deep into the sand. They leave a most distinctive keyhole-shape impression at the mouths of their burrows. The best razorfish beds are to be found below the normal low water mark and are often only available on spring tides. A thin metre-long bar with an arrowhead at the point is inserted into the hole and through the razorfish; a full twist and the impaled animal may be lifted from its burrow. They are excellent bait and may be used whole or in segments. They are soft bait and the most dependable method of hooking is again through the 'foot'.

Cockles and clams are also quite good bait and their preparation is similar to that of the mussel.

Limpets are an excellent bait for wrasse but are little used for other species, although I have taken some good bass with them in the vicinity of rocky outcrops.

Fish baits

Fish or fish segments are a first class bait and are very popular with anglers because they are so easily purchased. However, the freshness of some of this bait can be suspect and although fit for human consumption, predatory fish may not be as easily convinced! The difference between really fresh bait and stale bait is the difference between haphazard bites and constant action. A wide variety of fish may be used as bait but the oily fish, such as mackerel, herring and pilchard, are by far the best.

The use of fish bait was originally limited to boat fishing but in recent years it has become increasingly popular amongst shore anglers. Whole fish are used for large predatory fish such as shark, tope and skate. Long strips or portions of fillets are used for other species. The bait should be prepared using a very sharp filleting knife as some fish prefer neatly cut segments of flesh. Others, such as ray and dogfish, seem little interested in the shape and are largely attracted by the smell or taste of the exposed flesh.

One rather bizarre fish bait, used along the Irish east coast, is freshwater roach. These are very oily fish and segments or whole fish are used to take a range of species including dogfish, ray and even tope!

Baits are generally mounted by sewing a single hook several times through the flesh and skin. When shore fishing, the bait can be secured using elasticated thread.

Mackerel heads and tails are excellent baits for conger, while the top half of the fish is an excellent bait for skate and the tail half an excellent tope bait.

Squid is another popular bait and may be fished either as strips or in the form of a triangular wedge. It plays a very useful role in night fishing for when used as part of a cocktail, its luminous glow attracts fish to the main bait above. Tipping with cubes or strips of squid is growing in popularity amongst both match and pleasure anglers.

Tackle adaptation

Sea angling, particularly from the shore, is a sport which can be enjoyed by all of the family. Unlike game and specialist coarse angling, which are largely male dominated sports involving long days of hard patient effort, summer beach fishing may be easily combined with a general family holiday. It does involve the location and collection of bait but this in itself may develop into an exciting adventure for younger children.

Specialist tackle is used by confirmed addicts, but it is surprising how many different species of sea fish may be taken with standard freshwater tackle and a little adaptation.

My own participation in sea angling started at the tender age of four, equipped with a light bamboo float rod which my dad had fashioned for me, and a small brass centre-pin reel. With this rather crude, but nonetheless effective, weapon I took small wrasse, pollack, coalfish, pouting, dabs, and even the odd adventurous plaice and flounder. This was replaced, at the age of ten or so, by a 9ft (2.5m) Greenhart spinning rod, patiently hewn from solid rectangular strips of the raw wood by my ever inventive dad. When completed, that rod was my pride and joy. Its dark varnished wood, rattling agate rings, smooth new cork handle and simple bright copper-coloured brass reel mount were dearer to me than any rod which I have since possessed. It stood the test of time well, and for six or seven seasons it performed admirable feats. In combination with my 30-shilling fixed-spool reel and standard 100m of 10lb (4.5kg) nylon, it landed for me a whole range of new species, including such admirable fish as a 3lb (1.5kg) codling and numerous school bass up to 2½lb (1kg). It even accompanied me on my first few inshore boat trips, but after much abuse and over-exertion it finally snapped while I was spinning for bass at the outfall of the Ringsend Power Station near Dublin (known to generations of Dublin anglers as 'the hot water').

Even the most basic equipment can be used to good effect in the sea. The average modern 8-9ft (2.5m) hollow fibreglass spinning rod, with a test curve of 12oz (340g) to 1lb (0.5kg), may be used for light ground fishing along beaches, estuaries, bays, and if you are extra careful, from a dinghy or boat. Float rods and strong fly rods are ideal for such sporting species as mackerel, garfish, bass, sea trout and pollack.

It is not primarily the size of the quarry which limits the use of light tackle in the sea but rather the different environment and the weight of lead required to hold bottom or fish effectively. While light tackle is fine under balmy summer conditions, it is certainly not recommended for a storm or surf beach in autumn or early winter.

When using such light tackle never be tempted to overtax the test curve of the rod by overloading it with standard 3 or 4oz (85–113g) sinkers fit for an 11 to 13ft (3.5–4m) beach rod, and three full hooks of bait. Not alone does such a rig make for difficult and dangerous casting but the rod will not have the required power to lift the lead and sink home the larger hooks.

Light bottom gear should be rigged using freshwater Arlesey bombs of 1oz (28g) to 1½oz (43g), a two-hook fixed or running leger rig, incorporating two size 2 to 4 hooks and small bait portions. With such balanced tackle the angler may cast 70 to 90m and effectively cover a far greater area of the seabed. Weed and tide may prove a difficult problem and if the sea is heavily laden with floating weed, struggling with a 70m 'clothes line' of such material may quickly over-tax the light rod. Better to wait for a change of tide and hope that the weed will clear.

Under suitable conditions be adventurous and do not be deterred from even the most exposed of storm or surf beaches. If bottom fishing proves difficult, try spinning or float fishing from adjoining rocks or piers.

Corrosion can take a particularly heavy toll of light gear designed for fresh water, and having returned home the angler should be careful to wash all tackle clean of sand and salt (see page 283).

CHAPTER 5

BONY FISH

Sport fish

Sea fish may be conveniently divided into two major groups: bony fish and cartilaginous fish or elasmobranchs (eg sharks, skate, ray). Deciding which species or family of fish to include under each subsection is difficult, since every individual species has something interesting to offer, either in terms of its biology or the specialist techniques required for its capture. However, the species which I have chosen to cover are first and foremost sport fish; that is, fish which are capable of putting up a moderate to strong resistance when taken on sporting tackle and, once landed, give the angler a sense of achievement. Secondly, the angling methods used in their capture will also take other neighbouring species. Fortunately, most sea fish are lavishly catholic in their taste and a range of species regularly comes the way of even the most dedicated specialist. The dozen or so sub-groups which I have chosen cover a range of common, shore, inshore and deep sea species and hopefully will whet the angler's appetite to seek out some of our more exotic marine visitors, such as halibut, mako shark, sea bream, hake and megrim.

Bass, mullet and shad

Bass

Origin

The sea bass *(Dicentrarchus labrax)* is a member of the great family of sea perch *(Serranidae)* which includes deep sea, inshore, anadromous and some freshwater species. Many, such as the North American striped bass *(Roccus saxatilis)* and the grouper of the tropical seas are much sought after as sport fish, and some attain weights of several hundred pounds or more. The bass occupies much the same ecological niche along the coasts of Europe as the striped bass on the Atlantic coast of North America. The striped bass, however, may live for forty years or more and attain weights of 100lb. The European bass is found in abundance from Scotland to the coast of North Africa and is most plentiful in the southernmost reaches of its distribution.

Growth rates

Irish bass are close to the northernmost point of their distribution and as a consequence are long-lived and slow-growing relative to their sun-loving southern brethren. For example, Moroccan bass may reach a length of 32in (80cm) at fourteen years of age while Irish bass would be in their mid-twenties at an equivalent length. Bass grow to a maximum weight of some 18lb (8kg) but the average weight is generally between 3 and 4lb (1.5–2kg).

Maturation and spawning
Bass are a voracious predatory fish which will feed on a whole range of sea creatures, including fish, sandeels, marine worms, molluscs, shrimps and crabs.

   Despite their voracious appetite, they are late maturing. Female bass mature at a fork length of 14in (35cm) when five to eight years of age, while males mature at 13in (32cm) when four to seven years old. Invariably, the larger bass (> 3lb; 1.5kg) captured are female. They spawn from April to July but the most common spawning period is mid-May to early June. They are fractional spawners and spawning may take place over a protracted period, as batches of eggs mature in the female's ovaries. Bass spawn in areas of swift tide and these strong currents quickly carry the fertilised eggs, and subsequently the fry, towards the shore. Here the young, one- to four-year-olds, are to be found in the lower and middle reaches of estuaries, in tidal creeks, lagoons, pills and backwaters.

Bass

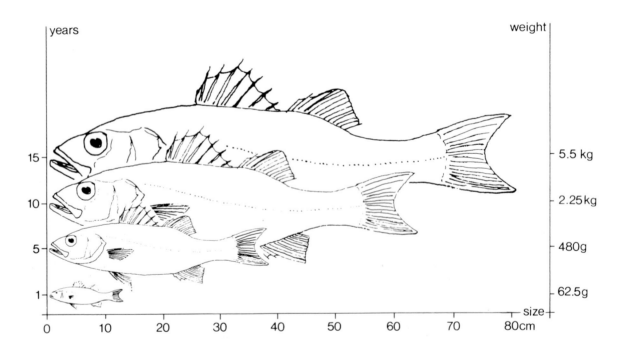

Irish bass stocks

Tagging experiments by the former Inland Fisheries Trust pointed to the fact that Irish bass stocks were exceptionally localised and that commercial over-fishing of bass would not necessarily be rectified by immigration from other parts of the coast. It was further pointed out that bass recruitment is dependent on exceptionally fine summers (eg summers of 1949 and 1959); as only finer than average years are good brood years, bass stocks are vulnerable. These reasoned arguments were largely ignored, and in the intervening years commercial netting has taken a heavy toll of some Irish bass stocks. However, the commercial capture of bass was recently banned and it is hoped that stocks will recover over time. One encouraging feature is the appearance of large numbers of 12oz to 1½lb (340-680g) school bass during the past year, which may indicate that the exceptionally fine summers of 1983 and 1984 have once again produced two good brood years and that these will contribute significantly to the recovery of stocks.

The majority of Irish bass are confined to the south-east, south and south-west coasts, but even within these areas they are not uniformly distributed. In their smaller sizes they are principally a school fish, but the larger specimens lead a more singular existence. They are very tolerant of fresh water and may be found feeding in the upper reaches of many large estuaries. When feeding in packs they do so most intently, carefully quartering every inch of the seabed. In addition to creeks and estuaries, bass are found along storm and Atlantic surf beaches, rocky headlands and amongst rough or broken ground.

Fishing for bass

Bass will accept a variety of baits but the most popular are lugworm, sandeel, crab and fish baits (principally mackerel or herring). When they are actively hunting small bait fish, the bass are taken by spinning. The most popular spinners include german sprat, Tobys, Tobis, wagtails and silver spoons. Spinning sandeels or mackerel strips will also take bass. At times of peak fish fry abundance, bass may mass or shoal off the coast (eg Splaugh Rock, Rosslare, County Wexford) and good numbers of fish are then taken by trolling.

Bottom fishing for bass is largely carried out along the storm beaches of the south-east and the surf beaches of the south and south-west. Bass are very sensitive to temperature and cease to feed at 8°C. The best shore fishing is from June to October along the east and south coasts while good bass fishing may continue until January along the warmer south-west coast.

The tackle used is that described previously for such beaches (see page 277). The key to success is simplicity, for bass are generally not very discerning, particularly in a good surf, and one-hook paternoster rigs are fished at distances of 30 to 80m from the shore. The most productive area along surf beaches is the second or third water table out from the shore. (To avoid the discomfort of a wet rear end, light body waders are a great boon when fishing surf beaches.)

The hooks used vary in size from 1/0 to 5/0, depending on the size of the bait. The best locations to fish are either end of the beach where rocky outcrops are likely to occur or at a point where fresh water discharges out onto the beach. The rod is held low, the tip slightly bent, exerting a fair degree of pressure on the grip lead. Bass will often sweep up a bait and immediately run shorewards, dislodging the lead and causing the loose line to billow towards the angler. There is little point is attempting to strike against these coils of loose line and the standard strategy is to run backwards up the beach, retrieving line as you go. By the time you have made contact with the bass he will be quite close to you and may react violently to the sudden pressure. If it is a big fish, be prepared for a strong lateral run through the shallows. Although normally associated with moderate to heavy surf and great crashing breakers, bass are often present along such beaches during relatively calm conditions. Long casting and the use of a running leger and fine leaders can pay handsome dividends at such times.

Night fishing for bass is very popular and the fish tend to feed actively from dusk until 1.00 am or 2.00 am and again around dawn. Bass fishing is normally characterised by short-lived periods of frantic activity as the fish sweep by, interspersed with longer periods of relative inactivity.

The September mist hangs low, wet and persistent over the village as we struggle with the parish priest's jump-leads. I anxiously look at my watch. The tide is low at 7.30 pm and we have little more than an hour's good digging before the tide covers the outer banks. Padraig dives into the driver's seat. One turn of the key produces little more than a low murmur. He curses loudly, a second, more persistent turn of the key and the damp engine reluctantly splutters and coughs its way into life. Triumphantly, Padraig revs the great old engine, black smoke billowing out of its exhaust. With much haste the jump-leads are removed, the priest's bonnet and doors secured and with a promise of a good bass for the tea, we are off.

Digging for lugworm is a warm, tiring business even in the cool weather of autumn. But when you are sealed in a thermal suit of light green plastic and digging against the tide on a Kerry beach on a drizzly September afternoon, it becomes pure hell. No time for the niceties of digging individual casts today, as we were late starting. We launch ourselves at the bank, laying open two ten-metre trenches adjacent to the area where the low sinuous lugworm casts are most plentiful. This is a wonderful strand, flat and well sheltered, it holds a prodigious quantity of lugworm, herringbone (or white ragworm) and razorfish. The really large black lugworm are only to be found near the low mark on extreme spring tides; however, these closer banks hold an abundance of moderately sized worms which I find more manageable than their larger cousins. Padraig swears by the bigger worms, particularly for large autumn bass, and maintains that they have yet to fail him.

Three-quarters of an hour's digging sees us both with a very respectable bucket of good quality lug. While I continue digging, Padraig produces the narrow, long cylindrical bar which he uses for gathering razorfish. Some 1m long, the tip is flattened in the shape of a flanged arrowhead. His tern eyes quartering the strand, he picks out the characteristically keyhole-shaped apertures of the razorfish burrows. The bar is plunged deep into the hole, twisted through 90°, and the impaled razorfish is drawn up onto the strand. Thirty minutes later and Padraig has collected almost two dozen razorfish, a fine haul by any standards. By this stage the tide has edged in over the lip of our earlier digging and is slowly seeping towards us. We decide that we have plenty of bait, for in addition to the lug and razorfish we also have some fresh mackerel which Padraig brought from the trawler the previous evening and some frozen sandeels which I brought with me from Dublin. Sandeels are an excellent bait and all the better for being collected fresh. However, sites for collecting sandeels can be difficult to find and their collection may at times prove problematical. I have found that freshly frozen sandeels are both firm and durable and an excellent substitute for the real thing.

It is 6.30 pm as we arrive at Brandon Bay. What a disappointment, the surf is flat and pathetic excuses for breakers lazily ease their way up the flat beach. Padraig suggests we head for home and an early night, but I am not to be deterred. Leaving my companion to take a catnap in the car, I rig my 11ft (3.5m) salmon spinning rod with a fixed-spool reel containing 200m of 12lb (5.5kg) monofilament and a single-snood leger rig. I slip a juicy lugworm, sand sack first, onto the 2/0 hook, and with a small bait bucket slung around my neck and a hand towel stuffed in my pocket, I head for the beach.

Equipped in this fashion and wearing light body waders, I am completely mobile and free to roam along the beach without the inconvenience of dragging a bag of tackle and a largely redundant 'jigger' (rod rest) along with me. I also have two spare 2oz (56g) bombs and a few hooks in my pocket just in case I lose some tackle, but this is most unlikely unless I encounter a large ray or tope.

It is now 7.00 pm and the tide is low shortly after 7.30. I wade out near to a tiny inflowing stream and

71

cast my bomb some 80 to 90m well beyond the second breaker. I then move the bait slowly along the bottom, searching for a quartering hungry bass. I fish for almost twenty minutes before I get a really good rattling bite, the rod buckles, I lift, and my heart sinks as I sense the sickeningly, solid, wriggly resistance of a lesser spotted dogfish. I winch the fish in, re-bait and cast again. Twice more I am taken by 1½lb+ (680g) LSDs. Time to move on.

I walk two to three hundred metres down the beach and wade out as far as I dare. The tide is just about turning as I watch my bomb sail across the flat blue sea. When my 30m wade is taken into account I reckon that the lead is a good 120m from the water's edge. I have not long to wait. The tip jumps twice in quick succession. I strike and a few minutes later a fine 1½lb (680g) flounder is mine. It gives me great confidence.

I quickly re-bait but this time I choose a sandeel. The fish is sewn tail first onto the hook and bound with elastic thread. Another long cast to almost the same point. I tighten into the lead and wait. I am just about to move the lead when, without warning, great billows of line roll back at me. Bass! I race backwards retrieving line as I go. After what seems like an eternity, I am in contact with the fish who is by now little more than 60m from me. Once I apply pressure he scoots laterally along the strand this way and that through the nearest water table. I pump him slowly towards the shore.

Once he feels the firm sand under his belly he races away again, causing the line to sizzle in the surf. Paddling madly with his great flat tail and fins, the bass disappears midst a vortex of sand and fine mud but all he succeeds in doing is neatly beaching himself on a small raised sandbar. Bending down, towel in hand, I gently but firmly fold back the shiny dorsal fin and grasp the 3lb (1.5kg) bass around the back. Turning towards the car I lift my prize high, gregging the wakening Padraig. He is out of the car in seconds and, giving the thumbs-up sign,

dives deep into the boot searching for his tackle. I hold the bass for several seconds in the surf while he recovers and marvel at the firm, strong musculature which I can feel rippling and pulsating under my fingertips. Two more, much smaller, school bass follow in quick succession; after this all goes quiet.

A westerly breeze which appeared with the change of the tide has by now begun to strengthen, the breakers are stirring in a much more determined fashion, and the stronger undertow is constantly uprooting my lead. I make my way back to the car and collect my 11ft (3.5m) beachcaster and multiplier reel. I attach a two-hook fixed-lead paternoster and a 3oz (85g) grip lead. On the 2/0 hook I mount a plain lugworm while on the larger 4/0 a mackerel strip, tipped with a cube of squid.

The light is beginning to fade gently as I join Padraig near the mouth of the small stream. He has had one small school bass but is delighted with the changing conditions and strengthening wind. 'If only I had a few of those large black *schnakes* (lugworm),' he complains.

I wade eagerly into the surf and cast 100m out beyond the second breaker. The Atlantic surf is by now at its best, churning, bubbling, sucking, slapping. It is difficult to describe the unique atmosphere of a live surf beach at dusk. The undertow slowly eats away the sand from under your heels and you slowly sink into a gravel grave of your own making. You move slightly to the left or right and the tide begins its task over and over again. The cry of the tern, the squawk of the herring gull, the fine surf spray on your face and hands, the rumble and rush of the breakers, all combine to stretch the senses to their limits. Close your eyes and drink in the taste, smell and soft caress of the sea. Clear your mind, revel in the emptiness and allow yourself to drift into a state of sensuous soporific contentment. Think of it as a vertical, fully clothed jacuzzi.

72

A bellow to my left jerks me rudely from my reverie. Padraig has hooked a large fish and is frantically moving backwards and forwards in the surf. The fish, not content with racing parallel to the shore, is also making mad dashes out into the churning surf. Padraig is desperately trying to gauge the fish's next move as he adjusts and readjusts the clutch to take account of the fish's weight and the draw of the undertow. After two or three minutes, the large fish has begun to tire and Padraig is finally in control.

I see little else of the battle, for my own rod jumps in my hand and a second good bass heads out from the beach. After a lively battle, I finally land a plump 2lb (1kg) fish. When I have returned my fish I make my way down the strand to admire Padraig's trophy.

A beautiful 5lb (2.5kg) bass, it is short, firm and exceptionally broad across the shoulders. Padraig has killed the fish to give as a present to our kind priest friend but ordinarily all of our bass are now returned to the water.

I return to my rod and remove one of the two snoods. In the dark I prefer to fish a single hook and a mackerel/lugworm cocktail on the larger size 4/0 hook. I also light the tilly lamp to aid with the unhooking of fish — particularly dogfish or ray, should they come our way.

We fish on until midnight. Periods of frantic activity are interspersed with much longer periods of inactivity as small groups of bass forage through the surf tables.

Mullet

The thick-lipped grey mullet (*Crenimugil labrosus*) is a member of a family containing over a hundred species. Its distribution is similar to that of the bass but the species is more tolerant of cold water and at times may be found as far north as Scandinavia, the Faroe Islands and Iceland. They are active shoaling fish and feed largely on planktonic organisms, snails and other invertebrates living among the seaweed and on various strands of plant material. To accommodate such a diet, grey mullet have a very muscular stomach and an exceptionally long intestine.

Spawning

Little is known regarding the biology of the grey mullet around the Irish coast. It is thought to spawn in late April or May, but spawning locations are still unclear. Its young inhabit shallow estuaries or bays and are often found in the company of young bass.

Growth rates

Mullet are exceptionally slow-growing, the average length-at-age being only half that of the bass. For example, a 12in (30cm) mullet is generally between four and eight years of age while specimen mullet of 6lb+ (2.5kg) are often aged at fifteen to seventeen years.

There is little commercial interest in mullet around the Irish coast and for that reason the stocks appear prolific. However, as with the bass, their age structure and exceptionally slow growth rate makes them potentially vulnerable to over-fishing.

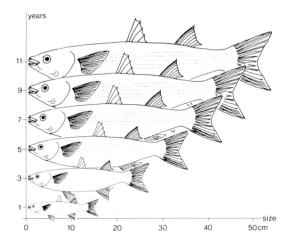

Open-sea mullet

Mullet shoals may be divided into two main groups: open-sea mullet and harbour mullet. Open-sea mullet spend their time at sea feeding on the tiny planktonic animals and plants which inhabit the surface layers of the ocean. They are frequently found in creeks and lagoons, moving about near the surface and displaying the arrowhead V-formation so characteristic of mullet shoals. However, they are exceptionally difficult to catch and show scant regard for even the most subtle of ground baits. They are silver, streamlined creatures and lack the depth and condition associated with the larger harbour mullet and are probably slower growing.

Harbour mullet

Harbour mullet are those which have become accustomed to the wasteful nature of human beings and are to be found in commercial fishing ports, marinas, and around effluent pipes of every imaginable size and description. They grow fat on such waste products and are much more inclined to feed on larger food particles. They are far easier to attract and a carefully concocted cloudy ground bait can quite readily hold a shoal for quite prolonged periods. However, despite their semi-domestication, they are still basically very shy, retiring creatures and are easily frightened or disturbed by the careless angler.

Fishing tackle

Pound for pound, mullet are amongst the strongest fish which the sea angler is likely to encounter. For that reason tackle should be strong and durable and no half measures should be taken in its maintenance and preparation. There are basically two types of rod which may be used for mullet fishing: a strong supple 9½-10ft (3m) spinning rod or a standard 12 to 14ft (3.5-4m) float rod. If you have a choice, avoid a tippy action in the float rod since a full action will ensure that a large mullet is subdued in a reasonable length of time without disturbing the remainder of the shoal. A fixed-spool reel containing 150m of 5-6lb (2.5kg) nylon completes the tackle.

Ground baiting

In harbour or pier locations the fish may be ground baited using a light, cloudy ground bait of barley, bran or breadcrumbs and containing particles of the food which the mullet are likely to be feeding on (eg bread, cheese, small pieces of fish). The ground bait should ensure healthy competition amongst the shoal without satisfying their hunger. The bait may be presented on a float rig, a fixed paternoster or a running leger, depending on the location and the depth at which the fish are feeding. They are principally creatures of warm summer weather and are most likely to be encountered from June until September. Float fishing is by far the most exciting method of taking mullet, as you can often see the fish take the bait. A waggler or slider is generally used with a strong size 8 to 10 hook attached. The depth should be varied until you achieve a situation where the mullet are constantly sucking or touching at the bait.

Serious mullet bites are very difficult to detect, a firm dip of the float may result in nothing more than a shot of adrenaline through your veins, while a slight tremor may provide you with a firmly hooked four-pounder. The upper thickened lip of the mullet contains extensive rows of sensory papillae, which the fish use to taste or test food. It is thought that many of the false bites are really part of a pre-biting tasting session. However, part of the thrill of mullet fishing is pitting yourself against such extraordinarily indecisive behaviour.

Hook baits

Hook baits are legion and include fish portions (flesh or entrails), cheese, ham, fat, bread, crab, macaroni, spaghetti, earthworms, maggots and even banana. When using cheese a good trick is to roll the soft cheese in strands of cotton wool so that it sticks better to the hook. Bread crust, flake or dough may also be used and one of the most exciting methods is to use floating crust and a controller float, in much the same way as one would fish for large rudd or carp.

Landing mullet

When landing your mullet you will require a large landing net, or more frequently, a dropnet. Remember that their large strong scales make these fish quite rigid and they do not fold easily into a net.

Twaite shad

Anadromous fish

A most interesting anadromous fish, the opalescent twaite shad (*Alosa fallax*) has only recently captured the attention of Irish anglers. It spends much of its life feeding at sea but enters large river estuaries, to spawn, in late April or May. A most enigmatic fish, its entry into brackish water seems regulated by both temperature and salinity. A really wet spring with accompanying floods can delay its entry until late May; equally, a severe spring can retard its spawning migration.

Location

Shad are highly sensitive to pollution and populations are easily lost. Twaite shad were originally present along all the east coast but are now almost confined to the estuaries of larger rivers in the south-east and south. Their distribution along the west coast may be more widespread than is known at present, since their furtive and clandestine entry into fresh water and their limited value as a table fish, means that their presence is probably not well recorded.

Spawning

Shad spawn in the upper estuary over a bed of fine silt or gravel. Not much is known regarding the fate of the fertilised eggs but it is thought that they hatch over a period of two to eight days, while drifting, and that the young frequent the middle and lower estuary until the autumn, when they too migrate back into the sea.

At the start of the spawning run small pilot shoals of predominantly male shad move up and down with the tide. These are later joined by shoals of the larger females. The males are mostly 10oz to 1½lb (280-680g) while the females may reach 2¼lb (1kg) or more. As spawning time approaches, the shoals show a greater tendency to remain in fresh water and may be seen resting in the deeper pools at low water. They make a most characteristic small dimple-type rise and at times may be seen splashing awkwardly at a passing mayfly or large sedge. Spawning takes place on a falling tide and large concentrations of fish are normally present. Even when actively spawning, both males and females continue to take lures, and it is not unusual to capture fish with milt or eggs dripping from their vent.

Growth rates
Recent work by scientists in University College Dublin has shown that shad are moderately fast-growing, with females averaging 13in (33cm) at four years of age and five-year-old males averaging a similar length. The larger fish are predominantly female, which may live until they reach ten to twelve years of age.

Fishing for shad
Shad are active predators and will take any shiny, flashy spinner, particularly bright silver. Amongst the most productive are small Tobys, Tobis, Krill and Mepps. In the larger rivers it may be necessary to cast 50 to 70m to reach the shoal and in such situations the addition of 1-1½oz (28-43g) of lead is often required. Sink-and-draw is a particularly effective method of retrieval. They will also readily take a silver lure-type fly and their antics on a fly rod have to be seen to be believed.

Tackle
The tackle should consist of a light, whippy 8-9ft (2.5m) hollow fibreglass rod and a reel containing 150m of 5-8lb (2.5-3.5kg) nylon. A landing net or dropnet is also useful, particularly if you are likely to encounter the larger 1½-2½lb (680g-1kg) females.

Shad fight exceptionally well and will both plane and jump. They have bony mouths and specimens often come loose during a strong tussle. They frequently exhaust themselves in their efforts to escape and should be handled gently and supported in the water for a few seconds before finally being released. Fish dumped straight back into the water will often lie dormant on the river bed for several minutes before finally limping off towards the parent shoal. I have my doubts that such badly shocked creatures survive the experience.

Pollack and coalfish

Pollack
Location
A fast-moving strong sport fish, the pollack (*Pollachius pollachius*) may be located at depths ranging

from 1 to 2fm (2–4m) to 20fm (40m) or more. It is often confused with its near relative, the coalfish, or saithe, but in fact the biology and distribution of the two species are quite different.

The pollack is found from the North African coast as far north as Scandinavia but is more common in the southernmost limits of its distribution. It feeds on a great variety of organisms including prawns, sandeels, marine worms, herrings, sprat and other small shoal fish. The pollack is not fond of cold water and will vacate its summer and autumn haunts to move into deeper water of 50fm (100m) or more in early winter. Here it spawns from February until April.

Shear rocky reefs and heavy kelp beds epitomise the classic pollack mark. Those located off the south and south-west coasts hold the greatest concentration of fish. They move onto such marks in May and although the larger pollack are not shoal fish, they remain in the company of the smaller pollack until late June or early July. They feed extensively on the large marine ragworm which spawn pelagically around this time. As such feeding becomes scarcer, the larger pollack move off the reefs in search of varying species of bait fish while the smaller shoal pollack are left to fend for themselves in or around the kelp beds. As the water becomes warmer, shoals of these smaller pollack move very close inshore and may be encountered along the back of piers and jetties, particularly where the water falls away steeply into 3 to 5fm (6–10m) or more.

Pollack are not fond of bright light and tend to stay deep, particularly during calm conditions. At such times they can prove very difficult to tempt out of the kelp but a light breeze and a dull sky provide excellent conditions for taking pollack at depth. Towards dusk the shoals move upwards in the water column and at twilight (so called 'pollack light') they may be taken on light gear at the very surface. Lures fished on a reservoir-type fly rod can be particularly effective at taking surface-feeding pollack.

Shore fishing for pollack

Shore pollack are not large fish (a 3–4lb; 1.5–2kg pollack is considered a good one) but they are particularly strong and their tendency to gather around the most inaccessible areas makes their capture all the more satisfying and exciting. Since pollack are normally taken closest to the thickest of kelp forests, a good strong rod and matching line are required if that first electrifying dive is not to leave your fish buried deep in the swaying undergrowth. A strong 9–10ft (2.5–3m) rod and 10–12lb (4.5–5.5kg) line are standard tackle for rock pollack.

Bait

The fish can be taken by spinning with german sprats, Tobis lures, mackerel feathers (baited or unbaited) and rubber eels. When using feathers, never be tempted to use more than two to three,

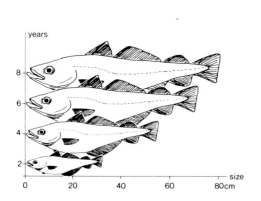

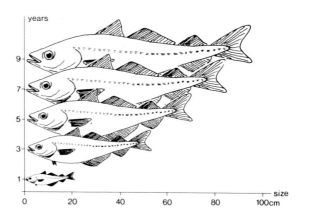

Pollack

Coalfish

since additional hooks will either foul the bottom or you will find five or six lively 1½ to 3lb (680–1.5kg) pollack impossible to handle. Pollack prefer a deep, slowly spun bait, particularly during the day, and it is often a tricky business to spin deep and slow without constantly fouling weed. Float fishing a slider float, a size 2 to 4 hook and a ragworm or strip of mackerel can be very effective and far less costly on tackle. If there is a good current along the rocks, you could also try drift-lining; live sandeel is a deadly bait if drift-lined close to the bottom.

Pollack as bait

Pollack are themselves an important fodder fish for many of the larger sea predators. I had first-hand experience of this many years ago while holidaying in Spiddal, County Galway.

Many Irish parents send their teenage children off for a month or more each summer to Irish-speaking areas along the south and west coasts. It is hoped that by surrounding the children with native Irish speakers, their fluency with the language will improve. I am afraid that my reasons for travelling to Spiddal had more to do with matters piscatorial than linguistic, but at least I did manage to learn the Irish names for all of the local fish species!

Having been caught by the local bailiff, on four consecutive evenings, fishing the lower pools of the then prolific but strictly private Spiddal River, I was banned from the river by the summer school principal. As a result I was forced to confine my activities to sea angling; no great hardship since the area abounded in the finest pollack and wrasse fishing.

During our final week at the college it was traditional for the brothers to organise a series of competitions for the students. Through hard, persistent pestering I managed to have a fishing competition added to the list of events. By the final Thursday I was neck and neck with another

79

Dublin boy, Ed Walsh, for first prize.

All of those who entered the fishing competition were permitted to fish for three hours each afternoon. The fishing areas were clearly defined and each competitor acted as a steward for his neighbour. The scoring system was five points per fish and one extra point for each full pound weight recorded.

On that Thursday afternoon we fished with a keen sense of urgency and by 4.30 pm we both had three wrasse of approximately 1lb (0.5kg) each. The competition was due to end at 5.00 pm and as a final resort Ed switched to spinning, hoping to take a good pollack and so clinch the contest. I decided to continue legering for wrasse.

As he sprung along the rocks he shouted across to ask if he could join me on my rocky perch. Convinced that he would quickly lose his spinner amongst the heavy weedbeds which lay in front of me, I beckoned him over enthusiastically.

Ed stood beside me and made a fine cast well out into the clear water beyond the weeds. As his spinner approached the bank of weeds his rod bent solidly. I smirked, convinced that the spinner was lost.

The 'weed' suddenly darted to and fro. My heart sank as I realised that Ed had hooked a good-sized pollack. He applied pressure on the fish, holding him hard and forcing him back from the impenetrable mass of weed which now lay below the fish.

Without warning, a menacing bluey-black tail appeared above the surface of the water, some fifty metres away from the struggling pollack. The 'shark' sped swiftly across the surface of the water and dived towards his prey. There was a terrifying pause while both of us stood spellbound and the rod was almost wrenched from Ed's hand as the 'shark' grabbed the hapless pollack.

Unfortunately for Ed, the nylon did not part and as the fish sped away, the pollack clenched in his jaws, yards of line spun from the gyrating spool. Tightening the slipping clutch Ed just hung on gamely. With a sickening jolt the main line parted and our 'shark' (or what I now believe to be a large tope) disappeared out to sea.

Boat fishing for pollack

Boat fishing for pollack may mean fishing at anything from 3 or 4fm to 20fm (6–40m) along a shear face. Indeed, the pinnacle of some excellent pollack marks may lie awash. The fish average 6–8lb (2.5–3.5kg) and standard or medium range boat fishing equipment is normally used (20–30lb; 9–13.5kg class rod and 20–25lb; 9–11kg monofilament) and the baits are larger versions of those used from the shore. The rubber-eel is a particularly effective bait, early in the season, when the pollack are congregated around the rocks feeding on the large *Nereid* worms. Deep, slow trolling can prove effective at this time and the use of downriggers for such fishing is growing in popularity. Drifting is also an excellent method and a large strip of mackerel is a favourite bait.

Pollack suffer the fate of many deep-water species in that their swim-bladder inflates as the fish are hauled towards the surface and although they may initially give a good account of themselves, the bloated sac eventually inhibits their movements. The use of lighter tackle has some advantages in such situations since the fish have time to adjust the gases in their swim-bladder as they are slowly pumped towards the surface.

Coalfish
Pelagic fish
Similar to the pollack in general appearance, the coalfish (*Pollachius virens*) is more rounded and less laterally compressed; it has an almost straight white lateral line and a rudimentary barbel. It is also known as 'saithe' and has a more northerly distribution than the true pollack.

Although a fast-growing fish — it can reach 24 to 28in (60–70cm) in its fifth year — it is also long-lived, and 51in (130cm) fish of almost thirty years of age have been recorded. It is a pelagic fish and like the pollack spawns at depths of 50 to 100fm (100–200m). Following the pelagic larval stage, the immature fish live relatively close to the shore. They first spawn at five to ten years of age.

Unlike the pollack, adult coalfish are gregarious and are found feeding together on shoals of fodder fish such as herring. Coalfish may undertake quite long feeding migrations and often follow herring shoals over very long distances. However, with the onset of winter, they abandon such preoccupations and make for the deeper-lying spawning grounds.

Fishing for coalfish
Coalfish are found over similar ground to that of the pollack and are taken by analogous tackle and methods, but at times during the winter months they may move close inshore and are taken by the winter cod angler. They are proportionately larger than the pollack and off deepwater marks may average 8–12lb (3.5–5.5kg). Younger coalfish, ¾–2lb (350g–1kg), forage along the storm beaches of the east coast during the winter months and make a welcome addition to the rather sparse variety of species to be found inshore at such times. With the growth of sea match-angling, the presence of small coalfish has become even more important as they provide the back-up weights and have assumed a role similar to that of the roach in freshwater matches.

They are an exceptionally strong hard-fighting voracious fish and, like the pollack, may be found at or near the surface at dusk. Larger coalfish are more nomadic by nature but are frequently encountered by boat anglers fishing deepwater marks for pollack.

Mackerel

Pelagic predator

A close relative of other great sport fish such as the tunny (*Thunnus thynnus*), the albacore (*Euthynnus alletteratus*) and the bonito (*Katsuwonus pelamis*), the mackerel (*Scomber scomber*) is a strong fast-moving pelagic predator, frequently reaching speeds of 10kmph. In summer it is best known for its savage and relentless pursuit of herring fry and sprat, in the surface layers of the ocean. At such times its own frantic behaviour and dense shoals attract large predators such as spurdog, porbeagle shark, tope and even large bass, coalfish, and pollack.

I previously dealt in some detail with the stock abundance and the fascinating mass migrations of the mackerel (see page 260) and so it will suffice at this point to mention a few additional features of the species' basic biology.

Growth rates

Mackerel is a fast-growing fish which attains 8in (20cm) at two years of age and 12in (30cm) in its third year. Mackerel are long-lived fish and specimens of fifteen to twenty years of age have been recorded. However, once they have matured, at the end of their third year, the growth rate slows down. A mackerel of 2lb (1kg) is considered a large fish but they can grow to 4lb (2kg) or more. They are prolific spawners and a single female may lay between 200 000 and 450 000 tiny pelagic eggs.

Feeding habits

Mackerel first appear off the Irish coast in early June but are most abundant in the months of July, August and September. As it moves from its southern breeding grounds, the mackerel feeds ravenously on the spring blooms of plankton, particularly on copepods and other small crustaceans. It actively sieves these creatures from the surface layers by straining the water through its fine gill rakers. As shoals of young herring fry and sprat begin to gather in mid to late June, the mackerel turns its attentions to harassing these tiny nutritious fish. This becomes the mackerel's main preoccupation until late September when the bait shoals disperse and they descend to feed in the deeper layers of the ocean.

A good sport fish

Mackerel are a common, ubiquitous species, frequently eaten by almost every family in north-west Europe. Perhaps it is because of this familiarity that many anglers have little regard for mackerel as a sport fish. They might well consider it an excellent bait for larger species but would never dream of hunting mackerel for their own sake. This is a great pity, for on light tackle they can provide quite exceptional sport.

Interestingly, it is not the great shoals of surface-feeding mackerel which provide the light tackle addict with the cream of his sport, but rather the small groups of individuals which hunt close to piers and rocky headlands.

For many years my brother and I fished religiously, at least once a week during the summer months, along the large deepwater pier at Dún Laoghaire near Dublin. At the very tip of the so-called West Pier is a flat, artificial platform of rocks and cement which borders a thick bed of kelp and bladder-wrack. Beyond the weed lies a bed of soft sand covered by some 5 to 6fm (10–12m) of water. At low water we would make for this shelf and fish german sprats well out beyond the weedy margin. Mackerel could be encountered at any depth from the surface to the sandy bottom. For two hours of the flood we would fish this mark and pick up a great variety of species, including two to six mackerel per session. These were surprisingly good fish, often well over 1lb (0.5kg) in weight and on light tackle they fought like demons. Getting them through the kelp was a most exciting and heart-stopping adventure, for our pocket money would barely stretch to one german sprat per month!

I have since learned that mackerel 'hotspots' occur at various locations around the coast, often in the most unlikely places. Local knowledge regarding such venues and of the time of the tide when they fish best can be invaluable to the occasional visitor. Later in the season the mackerel shoals can, at times, herd their unfortunate prey into estuaries, bays or along beaches and strands. Shoals generally arrive on an evening tide, particularly when high water corresponds with dusk. Such behaviour generally corresponds with the city dwellers' standard two-week August holiday and brings about a frantic feverish excitement which involves old and young alike. Every possible instrument is used as a makeshift sea rod, from antique split-cane fly rods to broom handles; anything which will accommodate a length of nylon and a hook. Shoaling mackerel are easily caught and are taken on live bait (often whisked by the bucket-load from the sea), spinners and lures, mackerel feathers, strips of mackerel, or mackerel skin, and even strips of silver paper slipped onto a hook.

However, this August madness often leads to the worst excesses and I have seen literally sacks of dead or dying mackerel left on the quays at Youghal where the participants, having discovered with some surprise the numbers of fish which they had accumulated, slipped some five or six mackerel onto a stringer and rather sheepishly made their way back to their caravan or rented accommodation; leaving the remainder of the catch to rot in its plastic coffin. There is no excuse for such mindless slaughter and it does little to promote sea angling as a family sport.

Boat angling

Boat angling for mackerel is generally carried out as a means of collecting bait for larger species such as shark, tope and conger. Mackerel feathers are used on a standard boat rod and these are allowed to descend quickly to the seabed. If mackerel have not been encountered on the way down, the feathers are worked up through the water column until the fish have been located. A streamlined lead is normally used so as to ensure a quick descent to the bottom. Strings of eight to twelve feathers are usual and when the quarry is finally located, a half box of mackerel can be taken in jig time.

A new type of feather rig has recently been introduced onto the Irish market. Traded as 'Hookai mini-baits' these incorporate a plastic, fish-like body, strips of fluorescent metal foil and a bunch of throat feathers on each hook. 'Hookais' are incredibly life-like in the water and although rather expensive are extremely effective at taking a whole range of sea fish.

But mackerel are not always easily located and a fruitless half day can be spent searching for them. Following a summer storm or continuing strong winds, the shoals may be dispersed and it can take several days of calm weather for them to re-form.

Locating mackerel

When searching for mackerel, there are various telltale signs, the most obvious of which is, of course, the presence of large concentrations of sea birds feeding avidly on the fry and smaller mackerel. Nothing is more certain to draw such birds as herring gulls, terns, guillemots, razor bills and even gannets away from the comfort of their rocky eyries as the smell and the sound of feeding mackerel. Shoals often leave behind evidence of their gluttony and the sea may be streaked with a mixture of fish oil, scales and tiny fish portions. Where large concentrations of fish were present, a heavy oily odour may be carried on the breeze for quite a considerable time.

Mackerel comprise a key component in the complex interacting ecological pool of fish which populate the North Atlantic. Many other species depend upon their legendary abundance as a principal food source during the summer months. It is no wonder then that anglers regard with some apprehension the massive commercial harvesting of mackerel stocks. Just what long-term effects could result from a significant, sustained reduction in the overall stock nobody seems willing to predict. Of one thing, however, we can be certain — such a catastrophe would have serious and long-term consequences for sea angling as we know it.

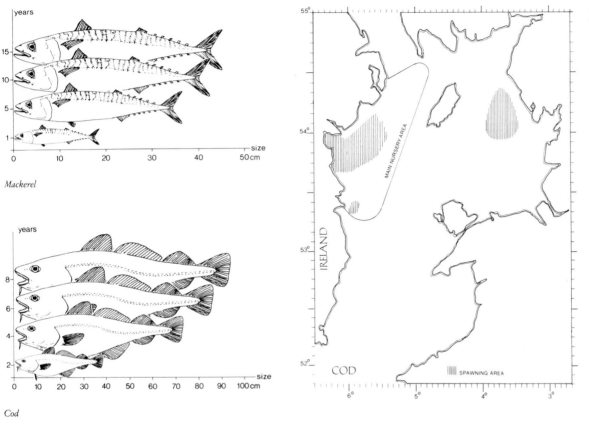

Spawning and nursery areas of the Irish Sea cod

Mackerel

Cod

Cod and ling

Cod

Cold-water species

Cod are a cold-water species preferring the colder climes of the far North Atlantic. There are three species: the common cod (*Gadus morhua*) and the two smaller species, the Greenland cod (*Gadus ogac*) and the polar cod (*Boreogadus saida*). As its name implies, the common cod is by far the most

85

abundant and forms the basis of the lucrative commercial fisheries. The great cod fisheries of the world are located in the Norwegian Arctic, north of Iceland, and in the seas between Greenland and Newfoundland. Even the North Sea cod fishery is small in comparison to the huge harvests taken annually from the three major stocks. Because of their economic importance, European cod stocks have been carefully studied. Some fourteen separate races have now been identified which may differ morphologically, physiologically or genetically.

Irish Sea cod stocks

Around the Irish coast it is only the Irish Sea cod stocks which have been studied in any detail. There are three largely separate cod stocks in the Irish Sea, one of which spawns off Carlingford Lough in the north-west Irish Sea, a second which spawns south-west of St Bees Head in the north-east Irish Sea, and a third which congregates west of Hartland Point in the Bristol Channel.

Tagging has shown that it is the Carlingford Lough stock which provides the autumn/winter cod fishing along the east coast. The Bristol Channel/Celtic Sea stock is fast-growing and may form the basis of the fine cod fishing which is available along areas of the south coast (eg Youghal and Cobh Harbours). We know nothing of the main Atlantic stocks off our coast except that in recent years they have provided exceptional winter fishing to some hardy pioneers fishing off the north-west coast near Killybegs. Consistently good bags of cod up to 33lb (15kg) in weight have been taken. Similar winter fishing is probably available elsewhere along the western seaboard for those adventurous enough to seek it out.

Maturation and spawning

Cod are an omnivorous, fast-growing species, some populations of which may migrate great distances to spawn or feed. The biology of deep sea and inshore races or stocks can be quite different. Some of the larger deep sea cod may not mature until they are six to twelve years of age while the inshore stocks may mature at two to four years. They are fast-growing species and may eventually reach a length of 5ft (150cm) and a weight of 90lb (40kg). They have a high fecundity rate and a female may release between 500 000 and 5 million eggs, depending on her size.

Boat angling

Cod are taken throughout the summer months while general boat fishing, but it is rarely that anglers fish specifically for them. The large cod are normally well dispersed at this time and are more often than not taken while drifting with a generous strip of mackerel. On light boat tackle they give a good account of themselves, but on heavier tackle they suffer from the same problem as so many other deepwater species in that their swim-bladder inflates when they are pumped quickly up through the water column and this greatly inhibits their freedom of movement.

Codling

In early September the codling appear in numbers at various offshore marks and these are avidly sought by both dinghy and shore anglers. Along the east coast codling generally run from 1 to 5lb (0.5-2.5kg) and anything above this weight is considered a true cod. In some of the north-eastern coastal districts of England where cod of 33lb (15kg) or more are regularly taken on rod and line (even from the beaches), any fish below 8lb (3.5kg) is considered a codling.

Codling feed best at dusk or the early hours of darkness and it is surprising just how specific codling marks can be: a short distance either side of the mark will result in little or no action, while the boat which is on the mark will hit fish on every drop.

Tackle

Standard light boat tackle is used with 1/0 to 3/0 hooks and heavy lead weights (6-8oz; 170-230g). The key to success lies in keeping the bait right on the bottom. Where marks are not known, it is advisable to drift until concentrations of fish are encountered, then anchor up, on or near to, the shoal. Baits include lugworm, mussel, crab and fish portions.

Winter cod fishing

The best of the winter cod fishing is to be had on the beaches of the east coast from October until January. It was originally thought that winter cod fishing in Ireland would never produce anything better than indifferent catches. However, consistent and patient efforts by a small group of enthusiasts have shown this not to be the case and in combination with small coalfish, school bass and the occasional larger one, east coast winter fishing is becoming increasingly popular.

Tackle

Winter codling are not exactly subtle feeders and the quantity of food they can stuff into their enormous mouths never ceases to surprise me. Never was the maxim 'a big bait for a big fish' more true of any species. Four or five lugworm, tipped with a cube or strip of squid on a 2/0 to 4/0 hook is considered a nice handy mouthful by a hungry codling. If only the smaller fish (1-1½lb; 454-680g) are running, the bait and hook sizes are scaled down accordingly. Because of their strong sucking mode of feeding, a good long snood (18in; 45cm) is called for. The larger fish will often take like a bass, sweeping hook, line and sinker up off the bottom with one great tug, causing the angler's line to billow back towards him in great unruly folds.

Success depends on getting the bait to the cod and holding it on the bottom. They prefer fast tides, heavy surf and a strong undertow. At times such conditions may require a 5–6oz (142–170g) grip lead and so winter cod fishing is no place for the enthusiastic amateur. Heavy autumnal seas, laden with drifting weed, will scoff at a salmon spinning rod and a 2oz (56g) lead.

Keeping the lead on the bottom is more difficult than might be imagined. Remember that a combination of tide, water depth and line bow are all acting against the inertia of the lead. Your aim must be to achieve the right distance, using good bait with a long snood and a large strong hook attached. A good firm anchorage is achieved by using a suitably shaped grip lead. Some experimentation may be called for before you achieve consistent success. The use of a heavy lead has one other advantage which is often forgotten: it travels more slowly through the air and a bulky bait is more likely to stay intact.

Despite the turbulent, confused seas of autumn, bait presentation should not be taken for granted. Some traditional anglers still prefer to use two- or three-hook paternosters, while the modern angler will choose a long snood, single-hook leger rig. There are advantages and disadvantages to both but in my experience the single-hook rig comes out best, particularly when night fishing. You can really load it with bait and when belted out into the darkness, there is far less chance of a disruptive tangle. In combination with a well-placed bait clip, the rig can be fished at various distances out from the shore. Cod fishing offers an ideal opportunity to test all of those gadgets which you have so fondly harboured in your tackle box all season. The constantly varying conditions will demand tactical changes: bite indicators, various forms of bait clips, patent plastic booms, sea adapted swim feeders will all have their moments. But do not think that the use of such gadgets is a sure recipe for success. They may help but there is no substitute for careful, intelligent bait presentation.

Night fishing
Night fishing for cod can be a cold, miserable, uncomfortable business if the angler is not well prepared for his 'ordeal'. Warm outer clothes, thermal underwear, a good dependable tilly lamp and above all a strong waterproof umbrella, make for comfort. You will find that the provision of such creature comforts, far from being a luxury, quickly becomes a necessity after two or three hours on a cold exposed storm beach which is being whipped by a gale force north-east wind.

Ling
Deepwater species
The ling (*Molva molva*) is the largest of the cod-like species and reaches a length of 6½ft (2m) and

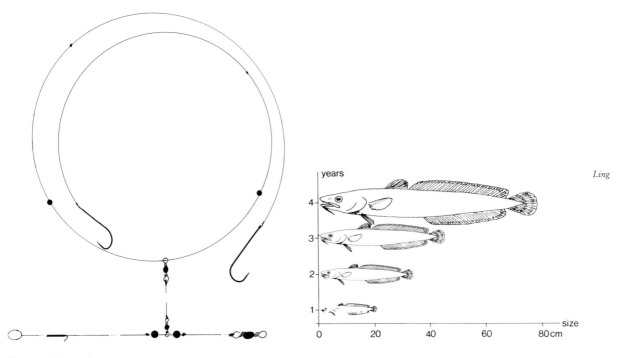

Ling

The increasingly popular
wish-bone rig

a maximum weight of 66lb (30kg). It is a true deepwater species and may be found at depths of 300fm (600m) or more. However, good quantities of ling up to 44lb (20kg) in weight are to be found around the Irish coast at depths of 20–60fm (40–120m).

Ling undertake long breeding migrations. Two major spawning areas are known, one south of Iceland and a second lying along the 100fm (200m) line which stretches from Norway to the Bay of Biscay. Female ling display a high fecundity rate and may release between twenty and sixty million ova. They are an extremely fast-growing, short-lived species of fish. Males rarely live beyond ten years of age but the faster-growing females may reach fourteen years.

Ling prefer high underwater reefs and rocks and are normally found amongst the roughest of ground. They are often most plentiful around wrecks and it is on such marks that most of the better Irish ling are taken.

89

Feeding habits

Ling are strong, powerful predators with a particularly fearsome set of extra fine teeth. They are mainly piscivorous and not too choosy regarding their prey. In the deeper areas of the ocean they are known to feed on blue whiting, octopuses and squid, but in shallow water they take a variety of fish including young pollack and coalfish, pouting, mackerel, flatfish and gurnard.

Fishing for ling — tackle

Ling are mostly caught during the summer months when general bottom fishing, and are often taken in the company of congers. For this reason, it is normal practice to use at least 18in (45cm) of 100–200lb (45–91kg) braided wire on the trace. A boom-type leger rig, 1 to 2lb (0.5–1kg) lead weight and a strong size 6/0 hook complete the standard terminal rig. General tactics for wreck fishing are dealt with in a little more detail in the following section.

Where congers are expected a 50lb (22.5kg) class rod and 50 to 70lb (22.5–32kg) main line are used but ling normally run in the 12 to 30lb (5.5–13.5kg) range, and where they are plentiful it is worth using a 20–30lb (9–13.5kg) class rod and 20–25lb (9–11kg) monofilament line. Make sure, however, to include the wire trace. On such light tackle, ling will give a far better fight and are less prone to swim-bladder inflation problems.

Conger

The conger (*Conger conger*), although outwardly resembling its close relative the freshwater eel (*Anguilla anguilla*), is a true marine animal, which frequents rough and rocky ground down to depths of 50fm (100m) or more. It is a fast-growing fish which reaches a length of 10ft (3m) and a maximum weight of 140lb (65kg). Some specimens have been known to reach a weight of 88lb (40kg) in as little as five years! It is principally a nocturnal predator and will take both fish and shellfish. The conger's diet is governed by his location but they principally feed on species such as pollack, coalfish, cod, lobsters, crawfish, squid, cuttlefish or octopus.

Maturation and spawning

Conger mature at five to fifteen years of age and when approaching full maturity the conger's body undergoes some dramatic and fundamental changes. Its digestive system and associated organs degenerate, its skeleton gradually becomes decalcified and it loses its teeth. Conger spawn in summer in a broad area of the deepest portion of the mid-Atlantic stretching from east of the Sargasso Sea towards Europe. It is thought that spawning takes place over depths of 1000 to 2000fm (2000–4000m). Conger spawn but once, and each female may release between three and eight million eggs.

The young pelagic larvae live at depths of 50 to 100fm (100-200m) for two years and having reached 5½-6in (14-15cm) they migrate towards the coast.

Fishing for conger — tackle

The conger is an exceptionally strong and tenacious adversary. When taken on rough ground it requires truly rugged tackle if the angler is to dislodge it from its treacherous rocky home.

Where large conger (40lb +; 18kg) are present, the tackle should consist of a 50 to 70lb (22.5-32kg) rod, 60-80lb (27-36kg) braided Terylene or Dacron line and a 12-16in (30-40cm) wire trace attached to a size 8/0 to 10/0 revolving-eye conger hook. A running leger rig incorporating two large, good quality swivels, a clements boom and a 1-2lb (0.5-1kg) lead weight are frequently used. The sinuous corkscrew motion of the conger will quickly knot both trace and main line if the swivels and revolving-eye hook are not included.

Landing a large conger will necessitate the use of a good strong gaff. Avoid any gaffs, no matter how strong, which have a screw-in type fitting. Once on board, the real contest may begin, for congers will often thrash and wriggle incessantly around the bottom of the boat. Their bodies are coated with profuse layers of slime and their antics often leave the deck in a dangerous and messy condition. To stun a conger, deliver a firm hard blow near the lymph heart, which is located just in front of the vent. Storing the conger in a large fish box with a well-fitting lid will avoid sliming of the decks.

A conger's mouth and jaws are lined with row upon row of strong sharp teeth. Be extra

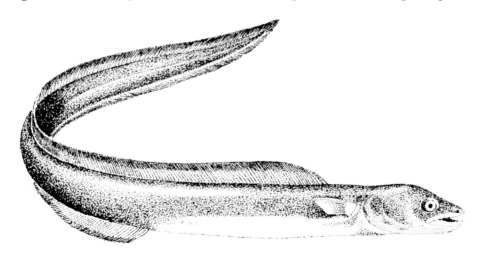

careful when dealing with these creatures and do not attempt to remove hooks and traces until they are well and truly dead. Conger can live out of water for very long periods, so be sure the fish is not just playing possum before reaching into his mouth! Before each trip construct a selection of wire traces, each carrying a strong link attachment. As deep-hooked fish are caught, the trace may be replaced and retrieved later from the dead eel.

Wreck fishing

Some of the best conger fishing is to be had off wrecks. Even relatively small wrecks provide an ideal refuge for shoals of small fish and protect them from the run of the tide. They in turn provide a plentiful food supply for larger predators such as the conger, coalfish and ling. Trawlers give wrecks a wide berth and an unfished site can provide really spectacular sport. I mentioned earlier the problems which may arise when wrecks are commercially gill-netted (see page 263) but thankfully such problems are rare at present.

Good wreck fishing is a product of the skipper's abilities and that of his anglers. Navigational equipment such as a Decca is essential for accurately pinpointing the exact location and lie of the wreck. The skipper must then position the boat so that his anglers are fishing directly into the scour. The tidal scour is a trough of sand gouged out under the sunken bows of the ship by the ebb and flow of the tide. It is the natural home of the conger.

Some authors maintain that monofilament rather than braided nylon should be used as a main line when wreck fishing. They contend that it is less likely to fray against the metal superstructure of the ship, less likely to twist in the strong tides and that the angler will find it easier to detect a bite. However, given the pressure which is exerted on the reel drum when lifting a heavy conger off the bottom, I would prefer braided nylon.

Hooking conger

A conger often seems to mouth a bait before actually swallowing it. Leave the bite to develop for a while before lifting into the fish. However, it is important not to delay too long, or the conger will have swallowed the bait completely. They invariably take a bait head first and so the barb and point of the hook should protrude out of the head. A whole small mackerel or half a large mackerel are normally used for bait. However, other small whole fish, such as pouting, whiting or pollack, work equally well.

You will notice that I do not use the term 'strike' when describing hooking a conger. The best tactic to adopt is to reel in the loose line, dropping the rod tip until it is horizontal with the waves, then lift the conger free of the bottom with one powerful motion. Your slipping clutch should be set so that it will release line only under protest; a large conger will invariably make a determined dive towards the shelter and safety of his lair. If the fish does manage to coil himself around a rock, a firm, consistent strain is one of the few options left open to the angler. A second strategy is to give a slack line just for a few moments and if you feel the fish move, to again lever him free of the bottom.

Night fishing
While conger are mostly taken from deepwater marks during the day, they are principally nocturnal feeders. This is seen most clearly around piers and promontories where fishing is confined to dusk and beyond. Surprisingly good conger can inhabit these areas, but the bottom is often strewn with rocks, old girders, cement blocks and thick kelp beds. Recovering large conger from such a morass is certainly challenging, but the odds are most certainly stacked in favour of the fish. Strong tackle is required, such as that described for winter cod (see page 313), but do not forget the all-important wire trace. **Landing and subduing a conger in the dark is a major task in itself, but if the pier is strewn with dangerous objects, the angler would need to exercise particular care.**

Flatfish

Flounder
Inshore fish
One of the most ubiquitous of our inshore fish, the flounder (*Platichthys flesus*) is a lively, plucky little fellow which can give an excellent account of himself on light freshwater-type tackle. Although principally a marine species, flounder have a great penchant for brackish or even true fresh water and I have found them 11 to 12km above the tidal influence. They are to be found from the tidal zone to depths of 10 to 12fm (20–24m), but during the summer months they mostly frequent estuaries, lagoons and shallow bays.

Flounder are a relatively slow-growing, long-lived fish. They may reach a maximum length of 20in (50cm) and a weight of 5lb (2.5kg), although most flounders lie in the range of 10 to 12in (25–30cm).

Maturation and spawning
Maturity seems largely independent of size, the males maturing at three and the females at four (8–14in; 20–35cm). They spawn in 5 to 20fm (10–40m) of water between February and May. Females may lay between 400 000 and two million pelagic eggs, depending on their size. Like many flatfish,

the larvae commence life possessing a normal symmetrical shape but at 0.3-0.4in (7-10mm) the left eye moves across the upper edge of the head and the larva begins to lie flat on its left side. When metamorphosis is completed its left side has become the light coloured ventral surface while the right side darkens and develops into the top or dorsal surface. It henceforth adopts a demersal mode of existence. Reversed flounder with the eyes and darker colour on the left side are, however, frequently encountered.

Feeding habits

The young flounder, or fluke, as they are called in many parts of Ireland, feed on prawns, bivalves, gobies, ragworm and lugworm. The older flounder also include crab, molluscs and small fish in their diet. They are principally nocturnal feeders and are often found buried in the sand during the daylight hours.

Fishing for flounder

Flounder fishing is at its best during May and June when the fish have fully recovered from spawning. They are curious, lively fish and will quickly investigate any unusual disturbance in the sand. Like the freshwater bream, they are captivated by a consistent series of sandy puffs as a bait or lead

Baited spoon rig

Flounder

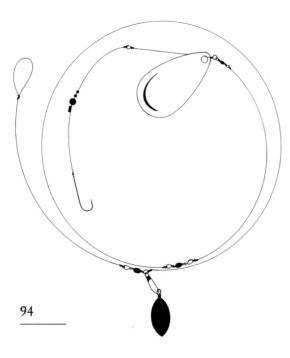

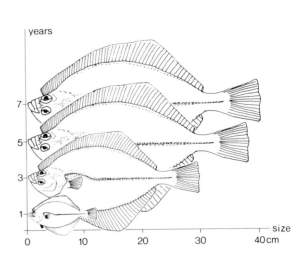

94

weight is drawn through the sand. Anglers have for many years capitalised on this fact and the baited spoon is one of the most popular methods of fishing for flounder. The rig consists of a 3 to 5ft (1-1.5m) length of 8-10lb (3.5-4.5kg) nylon attached via a snap swivel to the main line. A 1 to 2oz (28-56g) Arlesey bomb is connected to the link swivel and a 1-3in (2.5-7.5cm) spoon is tied onto the trace approximately 12in (30cm) above the size 4-1/0 hook. Some authorities recommend inserting a swivel below the spoon to ensure that the bait does not revolve or spin.

The rig is cast out and allowed to settle on the bottom. It is then swept along the seabed for 1.5 to 2m by drawing the rod horizontally to the left or right. It is allowed to settle as line is retrieved and then the process is repeated. A flounder will normally take the bait just as it starts to move along the bottom. Give him a few seconds to take hold of the bait and then strike firmly. The choice of bait will depend on location, but lugworm, ragworm or small fish baits are probably best with the baited spoon. At low water, flounders are concentrated into the creeks and lagoons which drain flat shallow estuaries. It pays to fish such locations at this time, but be aware that flounders prefer the banks and shallows, not the deeper gullies.

By fishing either a baited spoon or a fixed paternoster rig on very light tackle, you may encounter some surprisingly good fish, especially on evening tides. Keep the bait moving and if using the fixed paternoster rig, include some small brightly coloured beads along the snood. A small lead shot or a leger stop placed some 3 to 4in (7.5-10cm) above the eye of the hook will ensure that the beads do not drop down over its eye. When really plentiful, flounder may be taken two or three at a time on a fixed paternoster.

Good flounder are also to be found amongst the surf tables of the bass beaches. They prefer clear unmuddied water and will quickly disappear if a strong undertow develops. Although a very welcome addition to a day's beach fishing, the flounder is only capable of a token resistance on even moderately strong beach tackle.

Plaice

Unlike the flounder, the plaice (*Pleuronectes platessa*) prefers deeper water and the bigger specimens are generally found over mussel beds or sandbanks at depths of 5 to 25fm (10-50m), but they have been recorded at 100fm (200m). Plaice is a long-lived species and some specimens of thirty to forty years of age have been recorded. In Irish waters, however, the females may live until the age of twenty-five but the males rarely live beyond ten or eleven years.

Maturation and spawning

Plaice mature at two to six years of age and spawn during the winter months. They eat little during this time and spawning may take place from January until April or May at a depth of 10 to 20fm (20-40m). The number of eggs per female can vary from 50 000 to 250 000.

Plaice and flounder readily hybridise, producing a smooth-skinned intermediate closely resembling a plaice but without the brilliant vivid red spots. The young larvae hatch at 0.2in (6mm) and by that stage possess a normal symmetrical shape. After one to two months and at a length of 0.4in (10mm), the left eye migrates across the skull and, as in the case of the flounder, the fish henceforth lies on its left side, which forms the ventral surface of the adult fish. It is therefore described as a right-handed fish.

Variable characteristics

Various races of plaice may differ quite significantly in fin-ray counts or vertebrae counts. Their growth rate is highly variable and depends on such considerations as genetic factors, food supply and even temperature. Plaice populations from the Irish Sea have been closely monitored over a number of years and a growth chart for this stock has been compiled. Irish plaice may reach a maximum weight of 11-13lb (5-6kg) but generally run from 1-2lb (0.5-1kg).

Despite their reputation as a sedentary demersal species, plaice may undergo quite prolonged spawning migrations. It has been calculated that by using the midwater currents and only periodically settling on the bottom to rest, adult plaice may cover 18 to 30km per day. Outside of spawning time it has also been shown, in the Irish Sea, that feeding plaice migrate constantly, both north and south along the coastline.

Fishing for plaice

Immature plaice are frequently found in shallow inshore waters feeding on small marine worms and crustaceans. As they grow, their diet changes to include sandeels, bristle worms, cockles, mussels, and thin-shelled bivalves such as razorfish. Unlike the flounder, plaice do not feed on fish.

Larger plaice are generally caught from dinghies or small inshore boats while fishing offshore banks of loose coarse gravel or low patches of rock alternating with banks of coarse sand. Plaice are fond of mussel beds and seem to prefer this habitat to any other.

Bait

An erratically moving bait is most attractive to them and any form of visual stimuli (beads, spoons, painted leads, white booms) will ensure that they are attracted towards the trailed bait. Amongst the three best baits for Irish plaice are lugworm, razorfish and mussel.

Tackle

When fishing inshore banks at depths of 3 to 5fm (6–10m) relatively light tackle may be used, and although light beach gear is frequently called for, the larger plaice can be relied upon to give a dogged, determined fight. The majority of fish are taken on the drift but good sport can be had by anchoring off the mark and fishing either a fixed paternoster or running leger rig towards the bank.

Plaice

Spawning and nursery areas of the Irish Sea plaice

97

Plaice, in common with many other sea fish, are quite catholic in their taste and may be taken on some very unusual baits. This fact was really brought home to me when we first went to sea in Francie's 'Milk Float'.

Francie is a cousin of mine and like my father has a most unique way with anything mechanical. My father tends to regard Francie as his protégé for over the years he has supplied him with various bits and pieces of engines and tools so that he might indulge his latest craze.

During the 1960s, along the County Wexford coast, there were consistently good stocks of winter herring. Some of Francie's friends were involved in the fishing and inveigled him to become their mechanic and general handy man, servicing engines and helping to keep their boats in trim. It was not long before Francie decided to branch out on his own.

He bought a dilapidated half-decker for £40, assuring the owner that he was only interested in the scrap content of the boat. The wreck, for wreck it was, had been moored in Courtown harbour for almost five years. The engine was a write-off and the superstructure was half rotten. The main timbers, however, seemed sound. With his usual roguish charm Francie convinced a local building contractor to loan him a crane and some men to haul the craft onto dry dock.

Francie then set about restoring the boat. He haunted the local library, pestered the local boat builders and fishermen and wrote a long series of letters to my father seeking information on boat building and the intricacies of marine engines. Well versed in all of the technicalities he eventually felt confident enough to venture forth seeking a re-conditioned engine, timber and paint. There was only one small problem — he had no money!

After several weeks of patient cadging he had obtained several cans of the ugliest green paint ever concocted, but little more. One evening a friend, who worked with a local creamery, mentioned to Francie that the firm had decided to concentrate on butter production and to abandon its involvement with liquid milk. There were several old lorries going for half-nothing, particularly one old van which the firm's tradesmen had converted for the transport of bottled milk, many years previously.

The next morning, bright and early, Francie was on his way to Gorey. The lorry was the answer to all of his dreams. The frame was made of plywood, the seats were good and the engine, although old, was still serviceable.

Francie soon struck a deal with the foreman; the lorry was his on condition that he paid back £5 per month, to the firm, over a twenty month period.

When we arrived for our holidays that summer, Francie could not wait for us to see his craft. He had finished work on her the previous November. Despite widespread local scepticism he had managed to repay the full £100 to the creamery and in addition to make a nice tidy profit over the winter months.

'The Milk Float', as she was affectionately named, was certainly the most unusual boat which the Irish east coast has ever seen. The superstructure, including the wheelhouse, had been repaired by the judicious use of the marine plywood from the frame of the milk lorry, the seats were bolted into the floor of the wheelhouse and the engine had been adapted by a series of the most ingenious mechanical rods and chains to turn the boat's screw or propeller. The original gear box was still intact and so a clutch and gear lever were installed adjacent to the wheel. The boat ran best in third although when the sea was really calm he had, on occasions, managed to reach fourth for short periods of time.

Francie was keen to bring us on a trip and my father needed little encouragement, particularly when Francie announced that he had a freshly dug box of worms on board. We loaded our light spinning rods into the boat and steamed out to sea.

Once outside the harbour Francie slipped the boat into second, then third and headed due south towards Cahore. Some twenty minutes after leaving Courtown he cut the engines and anchored the boat.

The three rods were rigged with paternosters as Francie regaled us with stories of his hair-raising exploits amongst the winter seas off the south Wexford coast. Finally we were ready and Francie produced his box of worms; not lugworms, not ragworms but large, juicy, black-headed garden worms from my aunt's garden! Stunned we sat there staring at the 'bait'. Francie chatted away happily as he impaled a large worm on each of the nine hooks.

'Over the side now,' he said. 'The flatties love these.'

And how right he was. For more than an hour we took beautiful plaice and dab and one rather apologetic-looking kamikaze dogfish. They did not seem to mind that the worms quickly died and shrivelled once exposed to the salt water.

Alas Francie had not made allowances for the ravages of corrosion and his engine only lasted a single year at sea. We had many more trips on 'The Milk Float' that summer. Although we subsequently switched to more conventional sea baits, none was as productive as the garden worms we used on that first session.

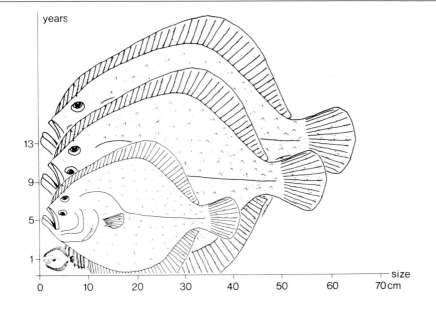

Turbot

Turbot

Turbot (*Scophthalmus maximus*) are true deepwater flatfish and although immature specimens may be taken occasionally from the shore, the larger adult fish are to be found in areas of strong current and lying at depths of 10 to 35fm (20–70m). They are fond of sand or gravel banks but may also be encountered amongst mixed bottoms of sand and rock.

Growth rates

Turbot are a relatively slow-growing long-lived fish and specimens of over forty years of age have been recorded. However, in general the maximum lifespan for a male is seventeen years and for a female twenty-seven years. They can grow to a length of 40in (100cm) but the normal range is 16–20in (40–50cm). Fish of average size are generally six to eight years of age. Young turbot, up to 14in (35cm), are generally found in shallow water but at four to six years they migrate to the deeper adult feeding areas.

Feeding habits

Turbot are principally fish feeders: some 90 per cent of their diet is fish-based, while the remaining 10 per cent is composed of squid, molluscs and prawns. They are particularly fond of the greater sandeel (*Hyperoplus lanceolatus*). They have a unique ability to blend in with the surrounding colours of the seabed, not simply by a change in general tone, but changing colour completely. This permits the predator to conceal himself completely from his hapless prey.

Maturation and spawning

Male turbot generally mature at the age of three (12in; 30cm), while females mature a year or so later at 14–16in (35–40cm). Around Ireland they spawn at depths of 5 to 20fm (10–40m) during the May to July period. At other points in their distribution they have a more prolonged spawning period from April to August. They display an exceptionally high fecundity rate and a female lays between five and fifteen million eggs. An interesting feature of all turbot populations is that males consistently predominate.

Commercial species

Turbot are a much sought after commercial species and in general a size limit of 12in (30cm) is applied to all commercial fisheries. This allows the maximum recruitment of three- and four-year-old groups into the population. Because of their relatively slow growth rate, stocks must be carefully managed if overfishing is to be avoided.

In Ireland turbot of 40lb (18kg) and over have been taken commercially but the rod and line record remains at 34lb (15.5kg). Irish anglers normally encounter fish in the 10-15lb (4.5-6.5kg) category, any fish above 18lb (8kg) being considered a specimen.

The best turbot fishing is to be had from August until late October. On the heavy tackle necessary for their capture, they could not be described as spectacular fighters but what they lack in sporting qualities they more than compensate for by their exquisite taste and flavour.

Favourable fishing conditions
Turbot lie on sand or gravel banks in strong tidal flows and at depths of 10 to 15fm (20-30m). They are large active predators which hunt by sight. They ambush their prey by camouflaging themselves on the bottom and waiting for some unfortunate creature to come within range. They will rise above the bottom to seize a juicy morsel and there is recent evidence to suggest that during the hours of darkness they actively feed off the bottom.

They take best during periods of settled weather and clear water. Turbot display little activity around the slack periods of the tide and are most active on the first run after low or high water. Of the two, the early ebb is the most productive, particularly if it coincides with a late afternoon tide.

Tackle
Because of the turbot's preference for areas of particularly strong currents, fishing is only possible with quite heavy gear. A 40lb (18kg) class rod and 30-50lb (13.5-22.5kg) braided Terylene or Dacron is often used. It is frequently necessary to use a 1 or 2lb (0.5-1kg) sinker to hold bottom. Turbot have sharp teeth and technically a wire trace should be used. However, they prefer a moving, flowing bait, and for this reason most anglers prefer a heavy nylon trace of 50-80lb (22.5-36kg) breaking strain. When the fish is hooked, the strong flow of the tide and the heavy resistance of a kiting turbot may fray even the heaviest monofilament, and anglers would do well to check their traces frequently. A leger or paternoster rig may be used and size 4/0 to 8/0 hooks.

Wreck fishing
One of the favourite haunts of really large turbot is the tidal scour along the hulls of wrecks. As the tide rushes along such hulls, it fashions the soft sand or mud into alternating banks and gullies. As described previously, the conger inhabits the depressions, at times resting right under the timbers of the sunken ship. Turbot, on the other hand, make full use of the sand and gravel banks, particularly on the leeward side of the wreck where they are generally most plentiful.

The rig used for wreck fishing is simplicity itself. A sliding boom is placed above a large swivel, onto which is attached some 6–8ft (2–2.5m) of 50–70lb (22.5–32kg) monofilament. The weight of lead should be sufficient to ensure that it lies securely on the seabed while the flowing trace is wafted about in the tide. Attached to the trace is a 4/0 to 6/0 hook, with a generous strip of mackerel attached. It is secured by the tail or narrow portion of the fillet which ensures that the 'wings' flap seductively in the current. To add that extra sparkle, some anglers attach a flashing attractor spoon 1 or 2ft (30–60cm) above the bait. Sandeels or other fish baits may also be substituted for the mackerel.

Hooking turbot
Turbot have a habit of tugging at a bait for quite a while before finally engulfing it. The best advice is to allow the fish plenty of time and if possible permit him to hook himself. When you have hooked the fish, particularly if it is a large one, keep a constant strain on the line for turbot are strong swimmers and can make full use of any lull in the pressure. Given any slack line, they will lunge uptide and generally succeed in releasing the hook-hold.

The skipper and his son Paul, a young chap of sixteen years, are already on board *The Cormorant* when I arrive at the quayside.

The fishing party consists of four people: myself, my regular fishing companion, Peter Holmes, and two experienced British anglers whose speciality, it seems, is deepwater wreck fishing. The skipper suggests that we take full advantage of their expertise and fish some deepwater marks. We readily agree.

The two English anglers prove to be both good humoured and modest regarding their angling achievements. Bert, the older of the two, is the owner of a charter service which specialises in deep sea angling off the south coast of England. Clive fished extensively all over the world. He is a keen competition angler and has won many prestigious prizes and trophies.

The sea is relatively calm, with just a light swell buffeting the port side of the boat. The one-hour journey to the fishing ground passes quickly as each of us in turn recounts fishing stories, theories and aspirations for the future.

As we near our mark, the skipper slows the boat until it is just making headway against the waves and he commences to echo-sound for the wreck which we are to fish. Twice he passes over the mark as he and Bert discuss their respective approaches to the fishing of wrecks. This particular ship had sunk some twelve years previously but the wreck had not been fished until the skipper had test-fished it with Paul some weeks previously. They had some exciting fishing but we are refused details until we too have fished the mark.

The skipper carefully anchors off the wreck so that the drift of the tide will lodge us immediately up-tide of its now well-charted position. Our bait consists of squid, mackerel and pollack.

Bert opts for squid while the rest of us choose to fish mackerel. The skipper suggests that at least one rod should fish pollack since it proved a particularly good bait on the last occasion the wreck was fished.

In deference to his wishes, Peter decides to fish a pollack strip.

My own tackle consists of a 30lb (13.5kg) class rod, 40lb (18kg) Dacron main line and a large multiplier deep sea reel. On the advice of Clive I choose a partial leger rig composed of a heavy monofilament trace attached to about 1m of 150lb (68kg) breaking-strain cable wire and a sliding boom which is free to run the length of the monofilament trace. Clive further suggests that my trace should contain at least three swivels since the corkscrew antics of wreck conger are guaranteed to twist and tangle any rig containing less than three large Berkley-type big game swivels. As an added precaution, I attach an 8/0 conger hook with a swivel eye attachment to the wire trace. Onto the hook I mount a mackerel head, complete with entrails.

We know by the echo-sounder that the wreck is lying in about 30fm (60m) of water. We can also see by the tautness of the anchor warp that there is a strong sweep of tide by the mark. I put on a 1lb lead weight in an attempt to counteract the speed and strength of the tide.

I lower the bait down towards the bottom. Eventually the line goes slack and I engage the spool and tighten into the lead. I can feel the rush of the current pulling strongly against the great belly of line and ever so slowly the bait begins to drag along the bottom. I can sense it moving and have just decided to reel in and re-weight the rig when my rod dips violently over the gunwale and I realise that I am in a good fish. Thinking that it is a conger I lift back hard in an attempt to force him clear of the bottom. The fish moves more easily than expected and suddenly I am playing a lively responsive fish. For the first 10fm (20m) or so the fight is all that one could have expected from a deepwater fish but as I pump my prize into the upper layers, he suddenly ceases to fight and I quickly force him to the surface. A fine ling of some 20lb (9kg) is quickly gaffed and brought aboard. It is obvious by his protruding eyes and swollen stomach that his swim-bladder has suffered the consequences of a rapid change in pressure and that it is hopelessly bloated. A few blows to the head and the fish is out of its misery. As Paul gingerly removes the hook, he pulls back the upper jaw of the ling to reveal the most awe inspiring array of sharp conical teeth. One look inside that predatory mouth and it is quite obvious why wire must be incorporated in all ling traces.

I re-bait my hook and lower it over the side. Within minutes I am fast into a second large ling. Clive and Peter are simultaneously into fish. As Clive pumps his fish hard towards the surface, Peter's fish bolts up-tide out of control and fouls Clive's line. An incredible and at times most amusing tussle ensues as both men attempt to play the two large fish simultaneously. Peter's fish is a 12lb (5.5kg) coalfish which refuses to tire. Clive's fish is a ling which seems quite content to be towed about by the frantic coalfish. Eventually both fish are boated and the men set about disengaging tackles and lines.

I am keen to tangle with a really good conger and decide that pollack strips are the answer. After boating a small ling, I change baits and lower it down quickly towards the broken shell of the wreck beneath. The bait has no sooner touched bottom when I sense the lead being lifted. I imagine it is the strong tide and jerking the rod up sharply, I retrieve some line. As I do so the rig takes off up-tide with tremendous speed. I tighten the drag and bend the rod into position. It turns out to be an exceptionally large coalfish which was quite willing to launch itself at the conger tackle. There really is no accounting for taste! When weighed, my coalfish draws the scales down to 14½lb (7kg), just 8oz (230g) under that elusive specimen weight. I change to a large red gill and for the next twenty minutes I enjoy exceptional sport hooking, landing and losing very large coalfish and pollack. I eventually change back to the conger rig and almost immediately take a 30lb (13.5kg) fish, my largest to date.

The wind has risen somewhat in the last hour and caused the anchor to drag. The skipper decides to lift anchor and re-position the boat. He suggests that the boat be positioned off the leeward side of the hull so that we can fish the scour along the side of the ship. Experience has taught him that large turbot thrive in such locations. They patiently lie on the sandbanks waiting for their prey to be swept by in the tide. We all readily agree and Clive demonstrates the turbot rig which he and Bert generally fish. It consists of a 6/0 hook, short 12-18in (30-45cm) wire trace and 6-10ft (2-3m) of 50-60lb (22.5-27kg) monofilament. The eddystone boom is mounted above the nylon trace and acts as a leger. When lowered onto the seabed the angler allows some 20m of line to pass through the sliding boom rig so that the mackerel strip is flowing gently in the tide, just off the bottom.

Immediately after lunch the boat is carefully re-positioned and five turbot rigs are lowered expectantly over the side. I do not have long to wait before I feel that most characteristic plucking bite of the turbot. I give him plenty of time to take the large bait well down before striking. Turbot are strong swimmers and despite the fact that they lack the dash of species such as the coalfish or pollack, they can give quite an exciting account of themselves in a strong current. This fish proved to be no exception and eventually I boat a very handsome 12lb (5.5kg) fish.

Despite such an encouraging start, the turbot do not seem to be present in any numbers and only two other small fish are taken by Bert and Peter. The wind has by now shifted to the south-west and strengthened to force 7. The choppy seas make wreck fishing extremely difficult and quite dangerous since the anchor may shift and foul the hull of the sunken ship. The skipper decides to up-anchor and steam for port.

Wrasse

Wrasse constitute a most interesting group of inshore fishes which includes the common ballan (*Labrus bergylta*), cuckoo (*Labrus mixtus*) and corkwing wrasse (*Crenilabrus melops*) and the rarer goldsinny (*Ctenolabrus rupestris*) and rock cook (*Centrolabrus exoletus*). They show enormous variation in colour, particularly the cuckoo wrasse, where the female is generally orangy yellow with two to three black blotches on her back between the dorsal fin and the tail; the adult male exhibits the most spectacularly vivid black and blue striped patterns. Ballan wrasse combine varying shades of orange, yellow, brown and green, to produce a most intricate weave of vivid colours. The colour of individual fish may also vary throughout a season, depending on such factors as habitat, season of the year, age, the food which the fish is eating and the depth at which it is located.

Ballan wrasse

Ballan wrasse (*Labrus bergylta*) are the largest and most common of this group and are principally to be found amongst rocky crevices and ledges along the south, south-west and western coastlines. They live amongst heavily weeded rocky outcrops at depths ranging from 2 to 15fm (4–30m). They generally average 2–4lb (1–2kg), but fish of over 10lb (4.5kg) are certainly present in some areas. Little detailed work has been carried out on the growth and ageing of wrasse, but one specimen of 16in (40cm) was aged at twelve years.

Feeding and hunting

Wrasse have protrusible lips and rows of strong, conical, canine-like teeth set in their strong jaws. They can rasp from the rocks a great variety of sedentary shellfish and will also feed on crab, prawns and shoaling sandeel. In order to crush the hard-shelled animals on which they feed, they have an additional row of strong crushing teeth in their throat. These are the so-called pharyngeal teeth. In the case of the wrasse they have been modified into several rows of rounded molar-like crushing teeth. They hunt during the day and retire to a rocky crevice to rest at night. Aquarium experiments have shown that wrasse may lie on their sides when resting and some researchers have claimed that they actually sleep.

Spawning

Ballan wrasse spawn between May and July. At this time the larger adults move inshore and it is during these months that really large wrasse are taken from the rocks. Wrasse form a nest lined with algae amongst the rocks into which are spawned a profusion of tiny creamy-white eggs. These stick to the walls of the nest because of the secretion of a thick glutinous mucus at egg release.

Locating ballan wrasse

The best ballan wrasse marks are invariably situated at the base of precipitous cliffs or rock faces. Hardened wrasse anglers thrive on the macho image which is associated with their sport and will often go to great lengths to scale the most dangerous faces in an effort to locate that ever-elusive ten-pounder. However, the average angler need not go to such lengths to enjoy wrasse fishing. It is true that some descents may be safer using a rope, but the use of full climbing gear and metal spikes is taking things a bit too far!

However, rocky ledges, no matter where they are located, are treacherous, dangerous places, particularly when wet. Leave the wellies and the waders behind and don a good strong pair of shoes, or better still, walking boots. Make sure that the soles are ridged and that they provide good strong support for your feet. There is nothing more uncomfortable than standing for a long session on rough, uneven ground wearing a pair of soft pliable shoes.

Wrasse fishing is generally a communal affair, involving four to six anglers. There are many practical advantages to a party of this size. First, it is safer; for the manhandling of tackle, food and accessories down a rocky path or along slippy ledges can be a dangerous affair for a party of two or even three anglers. Secondly, wrasse fishing is above all else fun, to be shared and savoured amongst friends.

Ballan wrasse do not swim in shoals but tend to congregate in groups of a similar weight. There are times when fish may average 3–4lb (1–2kg) and still rarer times when all the fish will be approaching 5lb (2kg). They thrive in warm Atlantic waters and are present along the shore from mid-May to mid-October. They love the power and turbulence of white water which often accompanies a large swell but are wary of storms and will move out into deeper water, returning only when conditions have settled down. Apart from spawning time, the really large wrasse are mainly confined to shallow offshore reefs where they are accidentally taken by anglers pollack fishing.

Fishing for wrasse

Wrasse may be taken on a whole range of baits, including lugworm, crab, mussels, limpets and even crushed periwinkles. They are fished for using a single-snood paternoster rig either on the bottom or on a sliding float. The rig is attached to either a 10 or 12lb (4.5–5.5kg) main line, which may be used on a light bass rod or a double-handed salmon rod. Where the fish are difficult to land in a dropnet, some anglers prefer to use a strong 15lb (6.5kg) main line and lift the fish up onto the ledge or cleft.

Fishing takes place amongst very rough weedy ground and so the use of a 'rotten bottom' type trace and disposable sinkers in the form of 1 to 2oz (28–56g) bolts or old spark plugs is most advisable.

To fish for wrasse with a paternoster rig, lob it out some 10 to 15m from your eyrie and allow it to drop until it touches bottom. At this point reel in any loose line and hold the rod horizontal and well out from you so that you can feel the sinker moving up and down over the bottom. You should not have to wait long until you feel the pluck, pluck, pluck of a good fish. When he gives a solid, determined pull, lift the rod and attempt to prise the fish clear of his lair. Wrasse are surprisingly strong and will make at least one forceful determined dive. If you manage to check the first dive the fish will normally come to the surface without too much fuss. However, should he reach the bottom he will dive deep in amongst the kelp and rocks and is almost certainly lost.

Wrasse slider rig

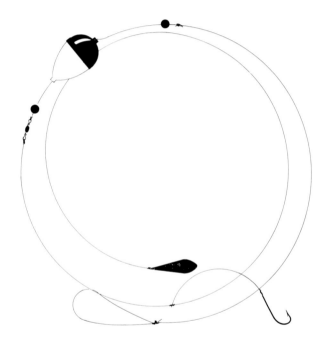

Wrasse suffer depth changes poorly and when taken quickly from even moderate depths can often suffer from a greatly distended swim-bladder. No matter how tempted you are, never poke your fingers into the fish's mouth in an effort to push its swim-bladder back into position. Those teeth were designed for crushing hardened shell, and finger bones are a good deal more delicate! If your catch is badly injured with a ruptured or greatly distended swim-bladder, you are well advised to tap it humanely on the head.

A slider float may also be used above the standard wrasse rig. A stop-knot or leger-stop is placed at the appropriate depth and a bead is inserted on the line to ensure that the float does not run down over the blood-loop. Float fishing is less wasteful on tackle and for my money, far more exciting.

Another method which I have found very useful, especially in areas of low rock where sandy patches are present amongst the kelp-covered rocks, is to cast the paternoster onto the patches of clear sand. If you can place the bait near the weed cover, it normally takes only seconds for a hungry wrasse to dart out and take the bait. Finally, a pliers or forceps is required to remove hooks from the toughened lips of wrasse.

Grey gurnard

Red gurnard

Tub gurnard

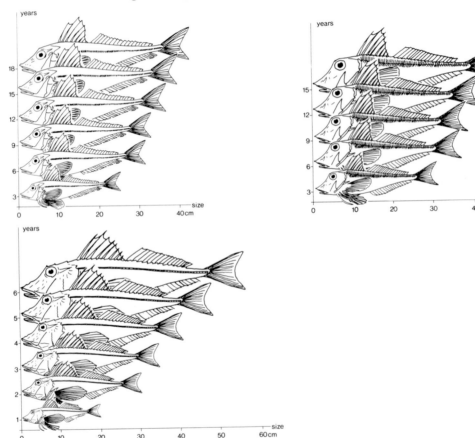

Gurnard

A most peculiar and strange group of fish, triglid or gurnard are widely distributed around Ireland. In the Irish Sea alone it has been calculated that the total population of gurnard weighs in excess of 3000 tonnes. Their odd triangular appearance is due to the large bony head, which is devoid of either skin or scales. Further armaments in the shape of short, sharp spines are present around the head, gill covers and dorsal fins. Their body is short and thin and tapers quickly towards the forked tail. They are predominantly bottom-feeding fish, and the lower three rays of the pectoral fins are separated into long finger-like tactile sensors. These are used to move the animal along and also to hunt out prey from the seabed. By using the separated rays as props, gurnard can gain a most advantageous view of their surroundings.

With the help of special muscles, which vibrate the swim-bladder, they can produce dull, growling sounds. Indeed, the term 'gurnard' comes from the French *grouger*, meaning to grunt. Recent aquarium tests have shown that gurnard make a series of defensive grunts when faced with predators or competition. It has also been suggested that grunting is used to locate mates and to hold spawning concentrations together at breeding time.

Until recently, little was known about the life history and general biology of Irish gurnard but thanks to the work of two scientists, Brenda Healy and Paul Connolly, based at University College Dublin, we now know a great deal regarding gurnard populations in the Irish Sea. With their kind permission I have drawn freely on their as yet unpublished information to give the reader some insight into the vagaries of this most interesting family of fish.

Grey gurnard

The grey gurnard (*Eutrigla gurnardus*) is the most common of our Irish gurnard and is to be found from the shallows into 75fm (150m) but it is most common at 5 to 50fm (10–100m). It is the gurnard which the shore angler is most likely to encounter. Not a very big fish, it reaches a maximum length of 16in (40cm). In most areas, anglers would consider a 1½lb (680g) grey gurnard to be a good fish.

Contrary to what was originally thought, the grey gurnard is quite a long-lived fish and many reach a maximum age of seventeen years.

Maturation and spawning

The males reach maturity in their second year at a length of 7in (18cm), while the majority of females are mature a year later, when approximately 8in (20cm). Mature females range in size from 6–16in (15–40cm) and release between 9000 and 200 000 eggs. Like the bass, they are fractional spawners (see page 294) and the breeding season may extend over a five-month period from April to August.

Feeding habits
Gurnard are principally bottom feeders and their main food items are crustaceans and fish. It has recently been calculated that in the Irish Sea some 60 per cent of their diet is crustaceans while 30 per cent is composed of fish. The remaining 10 per cent consists of a mixture of other benthic and pelagic organisms. Amongst the more common food items are prawns, shrimps, sandeel, poor cod, pouting and juvenile plaice.

Fishing for grey gurnard
Grey gurnard are mainly to be found over clear, sandy bottoms and are regularly taken by anglers engaged in general bottom fishing. Baits include ragworm, crab and small pieces of herring or mackerel, fished on either a fixed or legered paternoster rig. They are also partial to some fresh gurnard meat. Greys are fond of a moving bait and will take a spinner fished close to or along the bottom. Indeed I have taken many good gurnard by working a german sprat amongst clear sandy patches near the shore. They will also take a baited spoon, similar to that described for flounder (see page 320).

Red gurnard
Large red gurnard (*Aspitrigla cuculus*), that is to say fish over 2lb (1kg), can easily be confused with the larger tub gurnard. However, when the two are placed side by side, it is seen that the lateral line of the red gurnard is crossed by a series of narrow vertical plates, set in a V-formation. The tub has a most vivid, bright blue border to the tip of the large pectoral fin which is missing from that of the red gurnard.

Red gurnard are to found in depths ranging from 15 to 100fm (30–200m). In addition to sandy areas, they inhabit mixed or rocky bottoms. They reach a maximum size of 20in (50cm) but normally range from 8 to 16in (20–40cm). The average size is variable around the coast but even in the best areas, a two-pounder is considered a good fish.

They are a long-lived species, reaching a maximum age of twenty years and their growth pattern is similar to that of the grey gurnard. Red gurnard appear to be more catholic in their taste than either the grey or the tub. Their diet consists of 48 per cent crustaceans, 26 per cent fish and 26 per cent other benthic and pelagic organisms.

Maturation and spawning
The males reach maturity in their second year and at a length of some 9in (23cm). The majority

of females mature in their second or third years at a similar length or slightly less than that of the males. Fecundity is high and it has been found that a range of females measuring 12–17in (30–42cm) laid between 31 000 and 350 000 eggs. Their spawning season is confined to two to three months between April and June.

Fishing for red gurnard
The baits used for red gurnard are similar to those described for grey gurnard and fish are taken on general fixed or legered rigs. They will also take baited mackerel feathers fished close to the bottom.

Tub gurnard
The tub gurnard (*Trigla lucerna*) is by far the largest of the three common gurnard. It reaches a maximum length of 30in (75cm) but angling-caught fish are generally 12–24in (30–60cm) or 1–4lb (0.5–2kg). It is a strong active fish and at times may be seen jumping clear of the water. More commonly, however, it inhabits depths of between 10 and 75fm (20–150m).

It is a faster growing, shorter lived fish than either the grey or the red gurnard and its maximum lifespan is thought to be in the range of six to eight years.

Spawning
The tub is a multiple, fractional spawner and has a two- to three-month spawning season stretching from April to June.

Feeding habits
When available, the tub gurnard feeds largely on fish and over 70 per cent of its diet in the Irish Sea may be composed of sandeel, poor cod, pouting, young plaice and dabs. When bait fish are plentiful, tub gurnard will rise off the bottom and actively scavenge in the company of bass and mackerel.

Fishing for tub gurnard
Tub gurnard are a strong sporting fish which make optimum use of their large, expansive pectoral fins, the fight often seeming out of proportion to their size. They can attain weights of 10lb (4.5kg), but a 5lb (2.5kg) tub is considered a good fish. They mainly inhabit areas of sand or a sand/rock mixture and are taken on mackerel, herring, mussel, ragworms, crab, lugworm or gurnard meat.

Gurnard flesh is firm and palatable but is often infested by small white nematode worms. These are harmless to humans, if the flesh is well cooked, but their presence in the fresh fish can be very off-putting, even to the most ardent fish eater.

As we make our way along the wet roads through Kilcummin and on towards the Conor Pass I realise that as far as my chauffeur is concerned, rules of the road are for non-anglers — especially when you are thirty minutes later than planned. He does not cut corners, he dissects them. You cannot possibly negotiate small Kerry roads at 70mph unless you drive straight down the centre. Much to the annoyance of two bulk milk carriers, the postman, two old ladies on bicycles heading for early Mass and an astonished ambling donkey, that is exactly where the car stays.

The rain has now eased somewhat and as we move higher into the mountains, it finally peters out completely. A light westerly breeze develops and as the grey shroud of mist is hunted from the valley far below, we are granted a shielded glimpse of the tiny isolated lakes which constitute the upper reaches of the Owenmore system. They discharge via the river of the same name into Brandon Bay at Cloghane, an estuary which ranks amongst the finest specimen flounder marks in Ireland.

But our thoughts are far from flounders on this misty, changeable morning. Padraig and two of his angling friends have discovered a new and exciting rock mark near Slea Head, on the very tip of the Dingle peninsula. I am singularly honoured, for I have been invited to test the mark in the company of Padraig and his friends; the first 'outsider' to be so honoured. Two previous sessions have produced encouraging catches of large wrasse and mackerel but all are convinced that further fishing will result in a much broader range of species.

Having collected Michael and Larry in the village of Ventry, we make our way towards Slea Head and Dunquin. Somewhere south-west of Ventry Padraig swerves to the left without warning and darts down a tiny, narrow, untarred country boreen. The road finally funnels into a rough rectangular space, barely wide enough to turn an average car and perched on the very tip of a high craggy cliff.

My heart gives a jump. I am not over-fond of heights but very fond of rock fishing, and so far the fishing has always won out. But this? Padraig senses my apprehension. 'No problem at all, boy. Just a small bit of a scramble down a rope.'

The view is magnificent. Stretched out before us is the broad majestic Atlantic in all its autumnal glory. At the base of the cliff the craggy broken underwater pinnacles are slicing and dicing the broad powerful swell into a welter of giant puffs of creamy shaving foam. Far beyond the broken waves, just peering at us through the lifting mist, we can see the easterly sheltered shores of the Blasket Islands and directly across the bay Michael points out Canglass Point and Valentia Island, one of the original deep sea angling venues in Ireland.

I am ushered over to inspect the ropes. The first leads down some 6m to a surprisingly wide ledge, stretching 9m or more in under the cliff face. A second rope is attached to a large boulder conveniently situated in the centre of the ledge and this rope disappears over the edge, towards, I am assured, an even larger and flatter ledge situated immediately above the high water mark. The ropes had been put in place the previous evening by Larry and Michael, so as to save us time.

We don our wet gear and Larry shins down the rope to ledge number one. The gear is passed quickly down and Michael joins him. Larry moves on to the second ledge and Michael calls for us to descend. With Padraig above me and Michael below, I convince myself that I am quite safe. Once I start the descent I find there are a number of firm foot- and toe-holds, and I surprise myself by completing the descent quickly and efficiently. The climb to the lower face is equally uneventful, although the rope is damp from both the mist and the sea spray and I am warned to take extra care.

The flat granite platform bears all the hallmarks of a really fine rock mark. Measuring some $6m^2$ it is bordered on either side by areas of low craggy rock which are easily accessible from the platform. Michael and Padraig decide to investigate the two rocky perimeters while Larry and I choose to fish from the platform.

It is over a year since I have tussled with a good Kerry wrasse and so I rig a slider float onto my 11ft (3.5m) bass rod and multiplier reel. The tackle is rather heavy but sheer broken rock litters the margins immediately below the ledge, preventing the use of a dropnet. The ballan wrasse can regularly reach 5lb (2kg) or more along this coastline and a strong powerful rod is required to winch such creatures up onto the rocks.

As I mount a small, neat, succulent lugworm onto my 1/0 hook there is an excited shout from Padraig, and as I look to my left I see his rod arched into a lively bouncing fish. Larry and I rush to the edge of the platform as Padraig clambers about like a two-year-old amongst the slippery, treacherous rock. 'No wrasse this one,' he cries. It is obvious he is fast into a large, strong fish which is desperately trying to dive deep into the kelp and shattered rocks. A second cry from the far perimeter of the ledge and as I turn I see Michael lifting a fine wrasse up onto the rocks.

Padraig's fish has by now begun to tire and as we peer into the bluey-green water, a streamlined brown shape darts to and fro some 2m below the surface. Two or three minutes later Padraig is ready to land his fish. With the drag tightened and his thumb firmly clamped on the spool, he raises the rod, it buckles perilously, but a beautiful 5lb (2kg) pollack is eventually lying at our feet. A magnificent creature, its purply-blue back, brown flanks and large glistening fins sparkle in the rays of the watery sun. Taken on a slowly spun Abu krill, the fish had struck some 60m out from his rocky perch in an area Padraig always described as 'between the black and the brown'; that narrow margin where the thick black kelp and rock shelve suddenly into banks of fine sand and gravel.

I move back to my rod and complete my rig, inserting a leger stop 3m above the lead. I lob out the bait some 30m and watch curiously as the red and white float cocks and settles. As the strong tide moves it towards the rocks, it suddenly begins to dibble and dash about on the surface. Anxiously, I wait for that one solid dive of the float which will signal that the wrasse has taken firm hold of the bait. The float darts under, I lift the rod and sternly check the deep dive of the wrasse. A persistent fighter, the fish makes several more lighter dives before I have him at the surface. As he rises, I catch sight of a vivid blue fish, his flanks covered in a mosaic of jet black variegations. I lift the wrasse towards me and realise that it is not a ballan but a rarer male cuckoo wrasse, easily identified by his most characteristic appearance. I release the hook from his mouth and gently return the fish to the sea. I always feel that wrasse, particularly the more vividly coloured forms, appear incongruous against an Irish landscape and would look much more at home amongst the rich coral beds of the South Sea Islands.

I re-bait and cast again. This time the float dips and then dives almost immediately. I lift the rod smartly, the large wrasse does the unexpected and accelerates. My rod arches over but the clutch setting is a little too weak and the fish heads straight for his weedy lair. I lift hard against him and apply strain to his left, but the large fish is stuck solid. I point the rod towards the fish and tap the butt in an attempt to irritate the hook-hold, but to no avail. I slip the reel into free-spool and suddenly release all pressure, the wrasse responds in textbook fashion and darts free of the weed, pulling line with him. I immediately re-engage the spool and pump the fish free of the bottom. With the combined momentum of the fish and the pressure of the rod, the line slices through the fleshy fronds of kelp. After several further anxious moments, my prize lies gasping at my feet — a beautiful ballan wrasse just under five pounds and in prime condition. I pause for a moment to admire his magnificent yellowy-brown mottled appearance before slipping him back into the sea.

Four further ballan wrasse follow in quick succession and all are close to two pounds (1kg) in weight. Michael keeps pace with me on the left, while Larry has difficulty with dense clumps of wavering kelp and bladder-wrack which consistently snag his bait. He hooks several good fish but only manages to land one. Padraig, thrilled by his large pollack, continues to spin. Using a variety of baits, all fished at varying depths, he succeeds in catching several small pollack, the largest about 1lb (0.5kg) and four good-sized mackerel. These he retains, but all other fish are returned unharmed.

Time for a little exploration. Gingerly, I thread my way amongst the rocks behind Michael and head for the outer edge of the cliff. As I approach the perimeter I see that a broad 3 to 4m ledge follows the very edge of the cliff face. The ledge leads to a second platform of rock. I move out towards its edge and peer cautiously into the water which is some 2m below me.

At first glance it is as if the sea itself has changed colour and has adopted a blotchy, discoloured appearance. The seabed is composed of low, rough wedges of rock, thickly coated in part with swards of swaying bladder-wrack. Interspersed amongst the raised rocky ledges are avenues of fine sand and gravel. It is the sun's rays reflecting off these tracts of sand which give the water its distinctly opaque appearance.

I remove both stop and float and cast my one-hook fixed paternoster towards one of the clearer areas of sand. A poor cast, the 2oz (56g) bomb falls short of its intended destination and slips into a neighbouring gap which is densely covered in weed. By pure good fortune the bomb slips into the only clear area in the complete garland of weed. I decide to leave the rig where it has landed and tighten into the bomb. Much to my relief, a hungry little wrasse darts out from the cover of the weeds and devours the bait. I strike and pull the fish free of the weeds. The smooth bomb uneventfully sails through the weed and my rig is once again safe. I quickly land the small wrasse and cast towards a second clear area, and seconds later another wrasse is hooked. Four more ballan wrasse, all in the 1–2lb (0.5–1kg) bracket quickly follow. To my left is a large clear bank of sand which shelves away steeply into far deeper water.

I have just enough time to fish this zone before returning to my companions. A change of tactics is called for. I quickly replace the paternoster with a 2oz (56g) lead, a 1m trace and a bright new german sprat. Casting well out into the deep water I fish the spinner fast and slow, low and high, but to no avail. I am just about to concede defeat when my rod arches into a pleasing bow and the line tightens, but only for a few seconds before the fish pulls free. That fish took near to the bottom.

I cast again, but this time I permit the sprat to sink right down onto the sand. When the line slackens, I know that the bait has touched bottom and I slowly begin to twitch it, sink and draw fashion, across the sandy bed. It has gone but eight or ten metres when the rod buckles in my hand and I am hard into a strong mobile fish. He quickly moves off to the left and peels line from the loosely set clutch. All my senses scream pollack. The fish turns and heads inshore. I quickly retrieve line and I am forced to back away to stay in contact with the fish. He leads me a merry dance for several minutes hurtling about this way and that before I finally catch a glimpse of the odd triangular shape and large plate-like pectoral fins — a gurnard and a good one.

After several false attempts to land the fish I manage to pluck him from the sea. A solid 2lb (1kg) tub gurnard, he had fought like a fish of twice his size. I remove the hook from his mouth, taking great care not to impale myself on the sharp spines, present around the gill cover and base of the dorsal fin. A fine fish from the shore, I am now contented to make my way back to my companions.

CHAPTER 6

SELACHIANS
(CARTILAGINOUS FISH)

Evolution

It is difficult for us to accept that before the appearance of humans, some one million years ago, anything other than the most primitive forms of life existed on this planet of ours. However, if the cartilaginous fish which now inhabit our seas could recount its ancestry, it would stretch far back into the murky fathoms of pre-history.

Scientists tell us that primitive sharks probably first developed some 500 million years ago but it was during what palaeontologists call the Devonian era, 300 million years ago, that sharks as we know them first appeared. The flattened shark variants, which we now know as rays and skate, evolved approximately 200 million years later, during the Jurrasic period. By the close of the Cretaceous, 60 million years ago, the selachian's evolution was essentially complete and they were the most abundant creatures in the sea. Indeed, every extant family of shark alive today was represented, from the dogfish to the great white shark.

By all accounts, these primordial seas were no place for a careless dip. Fossil records show that the ancestor of the present-day great white (*Carcharodon carcharias*) was one of the largest predators ever to have lived. Its teeth were some 6in (15cm) long and weighed an average of 12oz (340g) each! It was between 24.5–36.5m long and a reconstruction of its jaws showed that when open they could easily accommodate six grown men. Modern great white sharks are a mere 9–12m long with rows of puny 2in (5cm) teeth!

Teleosts and selachians

It is estimated that there are some 40 000 species of fish alive today. Of these, the great majority are teleosts or bony fish and the selachians or cartilaginous fish are only represented by a mere 500 to 600 species.

Zoologists have divided fish into three major groups: the *cyclostomes* (including the lampreys and primitive hagfish), the *teleosts* and the *selachians*. The latter group is further subdivided into its two principal components: the order *selachii*, which incorporates all the true sharks, and the order *batoidei* which includes the skates and rays.

McCormick, Allen and Young, in their excellent book *Shadows in the Sea*, have nicely encapsulated in a table the essential differences between teleosts and selachians and with their kind permission, I reproduce it overleaf.

	Teleosts (*All Bony Fish*)	Selachians (*Sharks, Skates, and Rays*)
Scales	Usually large, rounded, bonelike in origin	Usually have denticles; actually tiny teeth
Gills	Typically, one on each side of head, covered by operculum	Typically, 5 to 7 gill slits each side of head, with no covering
Air bladder	Usually present	Never present
Reproduction	Usually by spawning; young usually hatched from eggs	Always by copulation; young of most species born alive
Anatomy	Skulls have sutures; teeth in jaw sockets; mouth typically at end of head; tail usually symmetrical, with backbone ending where tail begins	No sutures in skull; teeth not firmly attached to jaw; mouth typically under head; tail usually asymmetrical with vertebrae extending into upper lobe of tail

The selachian skeleton

The most dramatic and basic difference between selachians and other groups of fish is in their skeleton. True bone is never found in selachians and although the cartilage may be strengthened and hardened by the addition of calcium salts, the resultant substance is not classed as true bone.

Perhaps the hardest part of the skeleton is the teeth. These hard, enamel-covered structures are much harder-wearing than other skeletal structures and as a result, it is mainly through fossilised teeth that shark ancestors are known. There are three basic types of teeth: strong pointed forms, ideal for grabbing and holding prey; the classic triangular teeth with serrated margins, perfectly fashioned for slicing and tearing flesh; and the cusp-like flattened 'pavement' teeth so typical of skate and ray.

Selachians are primarily predators and frequently lose teeth when tackling large or tenacious prey. Such teeth loss is of no concern to the fish for their dentition consists of orderly rows of teeth, often numbering a 1000 or more. They are replaced by means of a somatic escalator or conveyor belt system which ensures that new teeth are always available to replace those lost or damaged.

Another extraordinary fact about the selachians is that their teeth are not confined to the jaws but are present throughout the shark's rough hide. These dermal teeth are known as 'placoid scales' or 'dermal denticles' and impart to the skin its abrasive characteristics. Shark-hide was once beloved of cabinet makers and from it was fashioned the first primitive forms of sandpaper (cf. *Shagreen*). In certain species of ray some of these denticles may fuse to form hardened thorns or spines.

Internal organs

Internally, shark and ray have a primitive digestive tract leading into an admirably stalwart stomach. Their super-strong digestive juices are well laced with hydrochloric acid and if spilled on the deck of a ship make short work of varnish or paint. They have no swim-bladder but their enlarged buoyant liver compensates for its lack. The flesh of selachians may contain high levels of urea, which leads to the rapid decomposition of the flesh. In edible species, proper draining of the flesh is essential prior to its cooking. When not hung correctly, ray is notorious for its ascorbic taste, hence the origin of the crude but descriptive term 'piss-ray' to describe freshly caught fish.

Respiratory system

Opercular or gill covers are missing from all selachians and respiration is accomplished through five to seven gill slits, located along their lateral margins. In some bottom-living species twin respiratory openings, called spiracles, are present on their dorsal surface, which ensures that the gills are not clogged by sand or grit. To breathe effectively, they must keep in constant motion, constantly wafting volumes of fresh aerated water over their gills.

Nervous system

The selachians are said to possess a primitive nervous system but like every other facet of their biology, it is marvellously adapted to its environment. The olfactory lobes of the brain are greatly enlarged and the shark's brain is known as the ultimate brain of smell. Although it hunts primarily by means of taste or smell, it can also see quite well, though it is doubtful if it can discern colours. It is well known that sharks have an acute sense of hearing and may detect water disturbances and vibrations at appreciable distances. Although their ability to hear as we know it is quite well developed, it alone could not account for the fish's uncanny sensory capabilities.

Shark are greatly assisted in their location of potential prey by the development of lateral line pressure detectors, a network of nerve tunnels which run the length of the shark's body and fan out on its head and jaws. In addition, many shark and ray also possess an array of pores, each leading to a network of sensory cells called *Lorenzini's ampullae*, first discovered in 1678. Each ampulla is filled with a jelly-like substance which reacts to either pressure or temperature fluctuations.

This primitive nervous system is extremely tenacious of life and stories regarding the ability of shark to survive horrific ordeals are legion. One record recounts that of a shark, caught, disembowelled and thrown back into the sea, to be later captured by the same angler who was using a section of the shark's own intestine as bait! Another angler, also with a penchant for disembowelling his catch, had a hand bitten off by a gutted shark.

Reproductive system

Selachians give birth in three ways: they either lay unhatched eggs (oviparous), or the eggs hatch inside the mother and the young are born alive (ovoviviparous), or the young are born alive having been nurtured via a very primitive placenta known as a yolk sac placenta (viviparous). The vast majority of shark and ray are ovoviviparous or viviparous. The number of young born is highly variable. For example, spurdogs normally produce three to four young but may produce up to twelve. Blue shark can produce twenty-five to fifty young and these may vary in length from 16 to 18in (40–45cm).

The oviparous species produce encapsulated eggs in the form of so-called 'mermaids' purses'. These are made of a horny, tough material, known as keratin. The surface may be richly variegated or plain in appearance and the 'purses' may be either oval or pear-shaped. Long flowing tendrils are present in each of the four corners and these are used to anchor the egg sac to rocks or store them on the seabed. They also assist the mother in giving birth, for she will frequently wrap them around anchorage points in order to give herself a purchase when discarding her burden.

Fertilisation is internal and the males of all species have appendages known as 'claspers' (or *mixopterygia*) attached to the pelvic fins. These grooved structures are used to clasp the female during copulation and are then inserted either singly or collectively into the female's twin reproductive openings. Seminal fluid flows along the grooves and mating may last for twenty or more minutes. In some species, the tips of the claspers are covered in hooks with which the male can lock onto the female. Nature, ever thoughtful, has ensured that the females of such species possess specially toughened skin around the vaginal area. Maiden selachians display a fine hymen-like membrane which may be used to differentiate them from previously mated females.

Regardless of the type of birth, a fully formed miniature adult results. There is no parental care, no puppyhood, no adolescence. A hungry relentless predator is launched into the sea, the latest descendant of a primal ageless breed.

Shark

Lesser and greater spotted dogfish

Two of the species most commonly encountered by the regular sea angler, the lesser and greater spotted dogfish, are included, not because of any great sporting qualities, but rather because of their increasing importance in match angling. Their abundance and ease of capture make them the ideal match species. It is mostly dogfish which provide the back-up weights in all major competitions.

The terms 'lesser' and 'greater' refer not to the density of spots present but rather to the average size of the two species. They both have rough, coarse skin, which can give the careless angler an extremely sore abrasion as the fish squirms and wriggles in an attempt to free himself. When unhooking a dogfish, it is best to have a soft cloth handy which will permit the angler to grasp the fish securely.

Lesser spotted dogfish (*Scyliorhinus caniculus*)

A hardy scavenger, the lesser spotted dogfish (LSD) roams the ocean bed seeking out food from every nook and cranny. It is a relatively small fish, normally averaging 1½–2lb (680g–1kg) and may be found at practically any depth from 30 to 60cm to deep ocean trenches. Little is known about its biology but it is thought to mature at 20–24in (50–60cm). It is an oviparous species and each female lays between eighteen and twenty egg capsules which are attached to weed by means of elongated tendrils. Egg capsules are laid in spring and the young dogfish take from eight to ten months to hatch.

Fishing for LSD

LSDs have been described by some authors as 'a pest', 'an abomination' or 'the bane of the sea angler's life'. This, in my opinion, is going a little too far, for although they have an annoying habit of appearing in vast numbers just at the wrong time, they can provide some sport on off-days, particularly along the beach. Their best attribute is the rattling great bite; once hooked they may be reeled in like the proverbial sack of potatoes.

They are to be found over most types of bottom but seem to prefer a mud/sand mixture. They are most active at night and feed on small fish, crustaceans and molluscs. They have a highly developed sense of smell and seem particularly attracted to fresh, oily fish baits or fish/worm cocktails. However, they are not fussy and will take almost any natural bait which the angler chooses to use.

Catching dogfish is easy; indeed the difficult task for the species specialist may be not catching dogfish. When match fishing, the ideal rig is either a fixed lead or leger three-hook paternoster. Under such conditions, catches of 100 or more fish for a two- to three-hour session are not uncommon.

Greater spotted dogfish (*Scyliorhinus stellaris*)

This is a much larger species of fish, averaging 8 to 12lb (3.5–5.5kg). It is also more localised in its distribution. GSDs grow to 25lb (11kg) or more but a fish over 16lb (7kg) is considered a specimen. Like its close relative, the LSD, this species is also oviparous, laying a series of black or brown rectangular egg capsules. The embryos are slow to mature, their actual rate of development being largely governed by the surrounding water temperature.

GSDs are large strong fish and fight better than their smaller cousin, especially when taken from a deepwater shore mark. They are primarily deepwater fish and prefer rougher mixed ground. They are quite good swimmers and feed on a variety of fish, crustaceans and other slow-moving creatures. They are taken when general bottom-fishing and are not specifically fished for by anglers.

Spurdog

Spurdog are amongst the most successful of shark families and representatives of the group are to be found in almost every ocean around the world. They are the most abundant shark in the North Atlantic and packs or shoals of spurdog, numbering from a few dozen to many thousands of individuals, may be encountered.

They are distinguished from other families by the presence of a poisonous spine in front of each of the two dorsal fins. Fossils of these durable quills have been recovered from Devonian and Carboniferous deposits. Known to palaeontologists as 'ichthyodorulites', some specimens have proved to be over 260 million years old. The larger dart-like quills were over 1m long and may have carried venom; modern spurdog spines are no more than 1–2in (2.5–5cm) long.

Growth rates

Spurdog (*Squalus acanthias*) normally average some 5–8lb (2.5–3.5kg) but they can grow to 22lb (10kg) and a length of 4½ft (1m). They are a long-lived fish, males may survive until thirty years of age while females live for a further five to ten years. Spurdog of seventy years of age have been recorded from the Pacific. Their initial growth rate is fast and they may average 16in (40cm) at one year old. However, once maturity is reached, at the age of five to ten in males and eight to fifteen or more in females, growth increments are smaller and a 32in (80cm) fish may be fifteen to eighteen years of age. Once mature they occupy unisexual shoals.

Reproduction

Spurdog are viviparous and each of the two female oviducts carries a transparent capsule holding between one and six eggs. Some three to ten embryos finally develop, depending on the size of the female, and the gestation period takes almost two years — the longest gestation period of any known animal. When the young are born the spines are covered by a cartilaginous cap. Once they have begun to swim freely, this covering is lost and a perfect miniature spurdog appears. Females display a preference for a rough substratum while males are usually found over a sandy or marly bottom. Females move inshore to spawn (or whelp as it is known), after which they encounter the males and are impregnated on their journey back to deep water.

Migratory species

Research by British and Norwegian scientists has shown that there are at least four distinct populations of spurdog in the north-east Atlantic. One of these over-winters off the south Irish coast and only in spring makes its way northwards towards the Barents Sea. In late autumn the spurdog return to their over-wintering grounds off southern Ireland. It has been known for many years that spurdog undertake long migrations and shoals frequently cover 10km or more in a day.

Commercial exploitation

Spurdog have been harvested commercially for many years in northern Europe, but their commercial exploitation around the Irish coast is a comparatively recent event. Dr Johnson defined oats as 'A cereal eaten by people in Scotland and by horses elsewhere'! So it was with spurdog, eaten in a few countries, despised in most. Marketing strategists decided that the term spurdog would be repulsive to the average shopper and so they were renamed *rock-salmon*. Their firm off-pink flesh added to the deception and a new desirable fish product was born.

Despite their apparent superabundance, there are many facets of the spurdog's biology which render it susceptible to overfishing. Its long lifespan, female maturation at eight years or older, two-year gestation period and the relatively small number of young produced all add to its vulnerability. There are growing signs that the Irish stocks are declining after relatively few years of commercial exploitation. There is also growing evidence that the tangle net (or gill net) fishery is selective for the larger female shoals of spurdog.

Feeding and hunting

Spurdog are often blue or steely blue-grey on the back and have the appearance of marauding, relentless killers — which they are. They are voracious feeders and will launch themselves at their prey with a single-purpose tenacity which has to be seen to be believed. When available, spurdog feed on fish — particularly shoal fish such as mackerel, herring, pilchard and whiting. They are also partial to crustaceans and a range of other marine invertebrates. When they move into an area in numbers, other species are quick to vacate the mark. They roam through all depths, feeding on both demersal and pelagic species of fish. They are to be found at depths from 0.5 to 80fm

(1–160m) or more. Packs of spurdog are often located in very definite areas and it is best to avoid these if you are interested in other species.

Fishing for spurdog

Spurdog are a lively member of the dogfish group and can give good sport, especially on light tackle. When feeding around the boat they are not difficult to catch and will readily take portions of fish or other natural bait on size 1/0 to 4/0 hooks. They have extremely sharp teeth but wire is largely unnecessary. A trace of 60–80lb (27–36kg) nylon will suffice but it may become frayed and need replacement after prolonged use.

Smooth hound

The smooth hound (*Mustelas asterias*) has become something of a cult fish in Ireland during the past few years. Its capture was originally limited to chance occurrences from the beach or boat but the location of inshore feeding areas along the south Wexford coast has resulted in a keen interest in its capture. The fish move inshore during May/June to feed largely on peeler crabs, which are at their most abundant at that time. They are taken by distance casting from the beach or from dinghies fishing close inshore.

Smooth hound are bottom-feeding shark with flattened teeth set in a symmetrical mosaic pattern and adapted for crushing such species as lobster, crawfish, crabs and molluscs. When feeding inshore, they are generally to be found over sand or gravel bottoms.

Reproduction

Not a great deal is known regarding the biology of smooth hounds but they can reach 6½ft (2m) or more in length. They are a viviparous species and the eggs are separated from one another by means of folds in the primitive uterus. They have a ten- to twelve-month gestation period and some twenty to twenty-eight young are produced.

Fishing for smooth hound

When beach fishing, smooth hounds are taken on night tides at distances of 80 to 150m from the shore. Normal bass-type tackle is used and the fish are taken on peeler crab mounted on a size 2/0 to 4/0 hook. The bait is normally fished on a running leger rig. The fish generally take the bait firmly and rush off on a long, hard, horizontal run along the beach. They are a very lively fish and a large smoothie (over 6lb; 2.5kg) may take quite a while to subdue. Although wire is not required, the trace should be of 20–25lb (9–11kg) monofilament nylon if it is to survive the crushing pressure of the shark's strong jaws.

Currently, the smooth hound season is short-lived and additional research is urgently required to trace the subsequent movements of these excellent sport fish.

Tope

Not much is known regarding the basic biology of the tope. It is viviparous and each female gives birth to between ten and forty pups. The young are born between June and September and may measure 16in (40cm) or more at birth.

The tope is not a very large shark, averaging around 20–30lb (9–13.5kg) but it may grow to 80lb (36kg+) and measure 6½ft (2m) or more. It is a bottom-living shark and is found in depths ranging from 1 or 2fm to 50fm (2–100m).

Feeding and hunting

A true fish-feeding predator, this slim-bodied athletic looking shark displays rows of finely hewn strong triangular teeth, which end in a point and are serrated on the hind side. Armed with such powerful weapons, the tope can efficiently seize its prey and quickly masticate it into digestible portions.

Tope feed principally on demersal fish such as small flatfish, pouting, whiting, cod and sandeel. Oily fish such as mackerel, herring and pilchard also figure in its diet. The tope is very much an opportunistic feeder and will also attack crustaceans, squid, cuttlefish and even fry where they are present in large concentrations. It is an able stalker as well as an accomplished hunter and will often lie in wait in narrows, especially where there is a strong tidal race, for its prey to be swept by in the current. In one celebrated location near Cromane in County Kerry, the tope gather in early May to feast on the descending salmon smolts from the River Laune.

Migratory fish

Experimental tagging programmes carried out by Irish and British scientists during the 1960s and 1970s have shown that tope may migrate unexpectedly long distances. Tope tagged off the Irish coast have been recaptured as far afield as the Porcupine Bank, the Azores, Gran Canaria, the Algerian and Spanish coasts of the Mediterranean, the north Spanish coast in the Bay of Biscay, off the northwest French coast and off the Isle of Wight. The greatest distance travelled by a tope tagged in Irish waters was some 3000km.

Fishing for tope

A much prized sport fish, the tope (*Galeorhinus galeus*) visits the Irish coast from May until September;

the best angling months are normally June and July. Most angling for tope is done over a clear, clean bottom, for the fish seem to prefer to hunt over sand or gravel. Relatively light tackle can be used and the tope's sporting qualities enjoyed to the full.

As a predator, tope will appear in numbers where the fodder fish are most abundant and while a general area may produce tope consistently from year to year, the actual marks may vary. Several blank sessions may be needed before tope 'runs' are located for a given season.

Boat fishing

When boat fishing, the angler should be well equipped with a light 20lb (9kg) class boat rod, 250 to 300m of 25-30lb (11-13.5kg) Dacron or monofilament, depending on preference, and a suitable multiplier.

Because of the tope's extremely strong, sharp, shearing teeth and rough hide, the trace should consist of wire, at least in part. There are two well-tested boat rigs, one of which includes an all-wire trace and a second which incorporates a section of strong 60-70lb (27-32kg) monofilament nylon. In each case the rig is attached to a size 4/0 to 6/0 hook, depending on the size of both bait and quarry. In situations where there is a good strong race of tide, slip on a sliding boom and release some 20m or so of line, then insert a stop on the line and release the rig over the side. The bait will then waft seductively in the current some 20m downtide of the lead. The weight should be sufficient to hold bottom and anything from 4 to 16oz (110g-450g) of lead may be required.

Baiting

The bait should consist of either a small whole fish (6-8in; 15-20cm) or a strip of mackerel or herring. Since tope fishing is normally done to an anchor and generally involves a long wait, the rod is placed securely against the gunwale with the ratchet on and the reel on free-spool. The slipping clutch should be carefully set so that once hooked, the angler can concentrate fully on playing the fish.

While waiting for that first strike, the angler should occupy himself by 'ground baiting his swim'. This is normally done by dicing up a few fresh mackerel or herring into small cubes which are cast over the stern into the tide at irregular intervals. It is surprising how effective this form of ground baiting or chumming can prove when tope fishing. The quarry picks up the oily scent well downtide of the bait and follows the line of freebies towards the hook bait, carefully quartering the ground as he goes.

A tope may take the bait in one of two ways: the line may suddenly start to peel free off the reel, in one long searing run of between 100 and 200m. This is the classic tope take. As the ratchet screams, the angler should lift the rod, switch off the ratchet and allow the fish to run unimpeded.

Carefully control the speed of the drum by applying thumb pressure on the rim from time to time. Like a large pike, the tope will run with the bait, then pause to turn his prey so that he is facing head first into his mouth and take a second run, devouring the bait fish as he goes. You may either strike towards the end of the first run or wait until the fish commences his second run. In the former case, you may miss some fish but the majority of tope are lip-hooked and play like demons. In the latter case you are almost certain to hook your quarry but the hook may be buried deep in the fish's throat. Since, as a conservation measure, all tope are now returned to the sea alive, there seems little point in taking a chance that the fish will be mortally injured by the hook.

The second, less common, type of take is where the tope lifts the bait and runs towards the boat. In this case it is better to retrieve line and wait until you feel the fish running against the line before striking. The strike itself is merely a matter of applying pressure to the rim of the reel and when you are in contact with the fish, sweeping the rod back in a smooth firm stroke.

Precautions

Tope are a very fast, active fish and when boat fishing it is good practice for other anglers to reel in their line once a fish is hooked. **The fish frequently dive under the hull of the boat and can create dreadful confusion and even danger if other lines become fouled in the trace or line, holding the dashing tope.**

Make sure the fish is well played before bringing him to the side. Formerly, tope were gaffed before landing but thankfully most tope are now tailed to ensure their safe return to the water. Use either a large salmon tailer or a loop of rope.

When you get the thrashing tope into the boat, beware of his dangerously sharp teeth. If he is deeply hooked, simply snip the wire as close as possible to the eye of the hook and let the fish off. Be particularly careful if he is hooked in the roof of the mouth, for the major veins and arteries leading to the brain are not very deeply buried in sharks and yanking at a deeply embedded hook may lead to a serious haemorrhage.

Tope may also be taken from the shore, but it can take several serious single-minded sessions before you encounter fish. Not alone are the shore marks a variable commodity, but the actual stage of the tide fished may also prove a vital component of success.

There are two principal shore locations where tope are likely to be present; along open, steeply shelving storm beaches, such as those located along the southern Wexford coast, and shear rock or cliff marks which shelve directly into 5 to 10fm (10-20m) of water. In addition, tope may take up station in areas of strong current or tide, particularly between headlands or in the narrows between an island and the mainland. Here again they may be accessible to the shore angler.

To tackle tope adequately from the shore, you will require the heavier beach/pier tackle described on page 274. Armed with a strong 11–13ft (3.5–4m) rod and 250 to 300m of 20lb (9kg) main line, you are still left with the problem of dealing with a sharp-toothed, rough skinned quarry who will make flitters of your line with one idle flick of his tail. The standard shore rig therefore incorporates 18in (46cm) of 40-50lb (18-22.5kg) cable wire and 2m of 60lb (27kg) monofilament. In the case of rock fishing for tope, distance may not be all that important and a gentle 30 to 40m lob may be all that is required.

Baiting and landing
The bait normally consists of a strip of either mackerel or herring bound by elastic thread onto a 4/0 to 6/0 hook. Small whole fish may also be used and these are mounted on the hook by passing it first through the open mouth and bringing it out half way along the body. The mouth should be pulled up above the eye of the hook and bound tightly to the trace by elastic thread. When rock fishing, some anglers prefer to use pollack or coalfish and they have enjoyed considerable success with these baits.

As in the case of boat fishing, the rod is left in a rest with the ratchet on and set at free-spool until the bait is taken by the fish. The first run can be even more dramatic than that experienced on board a boat and distances of 200m or more are often covered by the fish before he begins to slow down. Do not attempt to stop that first long streak but as the fish slows, apply pressure to the drum and lean back into the fish. If he is well hooked, the sudden shock of the hook going home may cause the tope to take off on a second long run. As the fish speeds seaward, remember to reduce the drag tension, as the combined weight and momentum of the running fish and the pressure from the great arc of line may overtax the main line or the hook-hold.

Let the fish play himself out in deep water and do not attempt to beach him until he is really tired. The fish may jump several times during the fight, particularly if he encounters shallow water. When he is ready to land, apply firm pressure and 'walk' him back up the beach in much the same way you would a salmon. The tope will generally follow like a dog on a leash, whereas if you attempt to play him to and fro in shallow water, he will thrash and dash about frantically and at some point his rough skin will almost certainly encounter your main line and part it.

Once beached, there is no need for either gaff or tailer, just lift the fish by grabbing hold of the tail and the dorsal fin. However, watch out for those sharp, gnashing teeth.

Rock fishing

When rock fishing, playing and landing tope can prove far more problematical and in such situations it is absolutely vital that the fish is fully played out before attempting to land it. A gaff or a tailer are invariably required and care should be taken to gaff the tope either at the base of a fin or under the mouth. Be especially alert when rock fishing, as handling and unhooking a lively 20–30lb (9–13.5kg) tope on a narrow rocky ledge calls for both confidence and calm nerves.

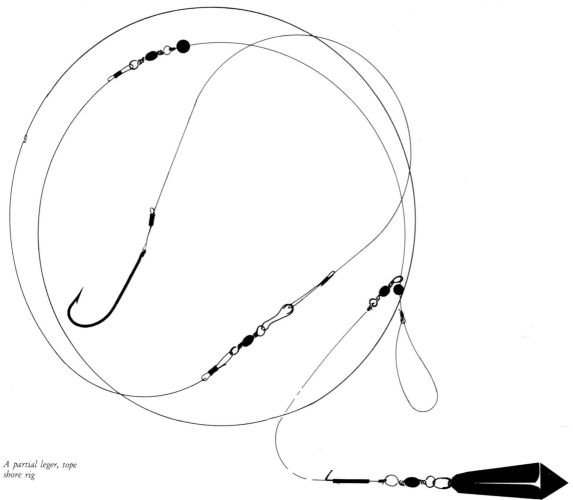

A partial leger, tope shore rig

The deceptive calm of the inner sheltered bay, where my boat is moored, has given way to a more pronounced swell as we pass the broken, craggy headland and head south-west towards the open sea. The sky has darkened since early morning and the wind is starting to freshen from the north-west. I am just a little anxious, for a tossing, stormy sea is no place for four men in a 5m open boat with a 15hp engine. The forecast, however, promises calmer seas and lighter winds for the afternoon. We finally drop anchor in an area which I have fished on several occasions and which I know to hold some excellent ray and the occasional tope.

Both Clive and I choose to fish for tope while the others gear up for ray. Although my tackle is rather heavy for conventional tope fishing, I know from experience that a medium to large tope can push the tackle to its limits, particularly when he has a good flowing tide to assist him.

For more than two hours Clive and I religiously adhere to hopes of a large tope while our friends enjoy some quite exceptional ray fishing. Using a peeler crab as bait, both blonde and thornback ray up to 14lb (6kg) are boated. The action is both fast and furious and although the average size of the thornback is generally quite small (4–5lb; 2–2.5kg), a change to lighter tackle ensures that they provide maximum sport.

Eventually Clive gets a good run on his mackerel bait but much to his disappointment, it turns out to be a lively 10lb (4.5kg) spurdog. Several other smaller spurdog are encountered and I move the boat some distance to the east in the hope of losing the shoal.

As we settle down on our new mark, I decide that a fresh bait may make all the difference. Choosing the largest mackerel I can find in the box, I mount a long, really thick, side of fish bait onto my hook. With the tail end well secured to the wire trace I drop the lead over the side and release line through the leger to ensure that the bait is flowing freely in the tide.

Putting my reel into free-spool and slipping on the strong ratchet, I momentarily leave my rod securely against the gunwale as I turn to place the remainder of the filleted mackerel into the box. Without any warning, the ratchet screams as a tope lunges at the bait located some 80m downtide from the anchored boat.

I grab for the rod and, slipping off the ratchet, allow the tope to make his first run unimpeded. The speed with which a tope can travel is truly amazing. The fish peels off well over 100m of line before his speed slackens. I engage the reel and strike firmly against the momentum of the moving fish. The tope spurts forward, rocketing through the water with a turn of speed and strength which I have never before experienced. Another 100m of line disappears from the reel and I am becoming anxious, for little more than 50m of line remains on the spool. With less than 30m of main line remaining, the fish slows slightly and rushes across and then against the tide. Madly retrieving my line, I somehow manage to stay in contact with the fish.

By this stage of the battle it is obvious that I have hooked something really special. All of the other lines are retrieved to give me free movement about the deck. Paul, Clive and Bert gather round me and, without appearing to instruct me in the art of the possible, they subtly offer advice and encouragement at each vital stage of the battle. With uncanny accuracy, they seem able to predict when the fish is about to falter or radically alter direction. With such accurate predictions of his likely behaviour available to me, I can pump the fish hard towards the boat or slacken off as the fish gathers himself for another long powerful run.

After what seems like an eternity, the fish is finally subdued and I gradually but firmly work him towards the boat. Bert grasps the trace with a gloved

Monkfish

Distinct features

This really ugly beast has features only a mother could love. Although a true shark, many of its physical features are intermediate between that of shark and ray. It is flattened from above with large expanded pectoral fins. These remain separated from the body and do not form a complete disc, as in the case of skate and ray. The mouth has moved well forward and is almost located at the tip of the head. The monkfish's squat, flattened features and unique behaviour make it almost impossible to confuse with any other species.

Although unrelated, the true monkfish may be confused with the angler fish (*Lophius* spp). This has little to do with physical similarities but is due to the fact that when sold commercially angler fish are often traded under the name monkfish.

Location

The monkfish (*Squatina squatina*) looks as if it is well adapted to life in the deep ocean, but actually it prefers shallow water, of 2fm (4m) or less. Monkfish are widely distributed along the south, south-west and west coasts. The two main fishing areas for really large monkfish are Tralee Bay and Clew Bay. Monkfish are frequently encountered by shore anglers fishing for bass, ray or flounder, but because of their fierce teeth and rough skin few are landed.

A tagging programme has shown that monkfish populations are localised and that although the fish may migrate into deeper water to overwinter, they maintain separate spawning populations. The fish normally migrate from points north to south during the autumn and make the return journey in spring. Monkfish stocks are easily overfished and this would indicate that the species is both slow-growing and long-lived.

Reproduction

The monkfish is viviparous (see page 344) and produces between ten and twenty-five pups, averaging 8-12in (20-30cm). The young are born in shallow water during the months of June and July.

Feeding and hunting
Their principal diet consists of fish, particularly flatfish, but they may also feed on squid, cuttlefish, molluscs and crustaceans. They are to be found almost exclusively over beds of fine sand and gravel. For such an awkward and ungainly looking fish, the monkfish is a very efficient hunter. It usually feeds on flatfish while lying half-buried in the sand, but it may also partially clothe itself in a coating of sand and lie in wait for its victims.

Fishing for monkfish
Monkfish are not exactly exciting fighters. But this does not mean that they can be easily subdued by the light tackle specialist. They are a heavy, powerful fish and once they have gathered momentum, monkfish are practically unstoppable on light gear, even when travelling at moderate speed. Monkfish generally average between 20 and 40lb (9–18kg) but grow to over 80lb (36kg).

Suitable tackle consists of a 30–40lb (13.5–18kg) class rod and equivalent breaking strain Dacron on a heavy duty multiplier. The trace consists of 8–12in (20–30cm) of strong 40–50lb (18–23kg) cable wire attached to 6ft (2m) of 60–80lb (27–36kg) monofilament.

Monkfish prefer large baits and whole mackerel or complete sides are often used on size 6/0 to 10/0 hooks. With such big baits, remember to leave the point of the hook unmasked. In addition to oily fish, monkfish will also take flatfish or whiting.

The angler may feel rather incongruous fishing in a fathom or two of water and only a few hundred metres from the shore, with tackle fit for deepwater wreck fishing. However, once he has hooked his first large monk, he will be grateful for the added security of the more powerful tackle.

Landing monkfish
Monkfish can often be hauled to the surface before they realise that something is amiss. At times, the fish are gaffed and on board the boat before the real fight begins. **Such situations can become dangerous, for 40lb (18kg) of snapping monkfish is a potentially dangerous passenger. They have rows of sharp backward-pointing teeth and can inflict really serious injuries. You are therefore well advised to tire your fish before landing him.**

When fishing from the shore, the tope rig shown on page 353 will fit the bill admirably, but if you are pier fishing you will require a good strong gaff to land your fish. Extra care is needed, particularly if you are attempting to gaff the fish off steps or from a slipway.

Blue shark
Although all the fish described so far in this chapter are biologically classed as shark, it is the larger

members of the group, often growing to well in excess of 200–300lb (91–136kg), which the average angler would consider to be true shark.

There are at least six such species which regularly visit the Irish coast: blue shark (*Prionace glauca*), porbeagle (*Lamna nasus*), mako (*Isurus oxyrinchus*), thresher (*Alopias vulpinus*), six-gilled (*Hexanchus griseus*) and the exotically shaped hammerhead (*Sphyrna zyganena*). However, only two of these, the blue and the porbeagle, are regularly taken by anglers. The arrival of blue shark off the Irish coast each summer is totally dependent on water temperature. They may appear as early as May, but in colder years their arrival may be delayed until mid to late June. It has been found from experience that there is little point in fishing for blues when sea water temperatures are below 14°C and that shark numbers increase significantly as the temperatures rise beyond 16°C. Of the remaining four species, it is the giant and athletic mako which potentially offers the most exciting challenge to the angler. It grows to well over 1000lb (450kg) and once hooked, makes frequent prodigious leaps clear of the water in an effort to throw the hook.

Open-sea fish

The blue shark is a sleek, handsome creature sporting an indigo-blue back, blue flanks and a most vivid enamel white underbelly. It grows to 13ft (4m) in length and in warmer seas has a reputation as a man-eater. In more temperate climates, such as our own, it has never been known to attack a person. The blue is a shark of the open sea and is seldom found in depths of less than 15fm (30m). It is a great wanderer, and journeys of over 6000km have been recorded. Some 6000 blues have been tagged to date off the Irish coast, and these have been recorded as far afield as Long Island (New York), the Azores, Halifax, Nova Scotia and the Bay of Biscay. Some prefer warmer seas and Irish tagged shark have appeared off the Leeward Islands, the Cape Verde Islands, Trinidad and even Barbados. One adventurous shark had travelled a minimum of 6035km and was at liberty for three and a half years; the longest recorded journey undertaken by an Irish-tagged blue.

Reproduction

Blue shark are viviparous, nurturing their young by means of a placental connection to a primitive uterus. Each female gives birth in summer to between twenty-five and fifty young and these may average from 14 to 20in (35–50cm). Blue shark become sexually mature at around 8ft (2.5m). The great majority of blues taken around the Irish coast are female. Although this has been known for many years, biologists have as yet been unable to explain this unusual phenomenon.

Feeding

The jaws of blue shark are lined with pointed, finely serrated teeth, and they feed primarily on

131

shoal fish such as mackerel and herring, but they may also take cod and squid. Spurdog also figure on their menu and blue shark are one of the few enemies feared by packs of these voracious predators. Blues are often accompanied by attendant pilot fish (*Naucrates ductor*) which hover about near the head of the shark. Blues feed primarily by means of a highly developed sense of smell and are thought to have poor eyesight. It was originally thought that pilot fish guided their mentor to his prey, but however appealing this theory may be, recent research has found little basis for it. Pilot fish are opportunists, feeding off scraps and morsels torn loose from their prey by the marauding shark.

Shark tackle

Since blue shark are taken in open water and rarely display the dash and vigour of the porbeagle, it is not necessary to use very heavy tackle. In Irish waters they average some 40 to 60lb (18–27kg) and any fish over 100lb (45kg) is considered a specimen. Fish of 200lb+ (91kg) are present but these are rarely encountered by anglers.

Standard shark tackle consists of a 30–50lb (13.5–22.5kg) class rod and a large multiplier holding between 350 and 450m of 30–50lb (13.5–22.5kg) Dacron. A butt socket is also used to land the fish but it is rarely necessary to include a shoulder harness. There are, however, advantages to using a harness, since it takes most of the strain and leaves both hands free to control the line and reel.

Shark traces are fashioned from soft, supple, cable-laid wire of 150–300lb (68–136kg) breaking strength. Avoid plastic-coated wire as it quickly chaffs once rubbed against the shark's rough skin. It looks unsightly and if salt water should lodge beneath the coating, it can lead to corrosion and rusting. The standard trace is some 15ft (4.5m) long and contains two or three large Berkley-type swivels. A hook length of 18in to 2ft (45–60cm) is attached to the lower link swivel and this leads to a size 9/0 or 10/0 forged hook. The hook length has a loop at the end so that it may be easily separated from the trace. The trace is fashioned from 150–200lb (68–91kg) wire while the hook length may contain wire of upwards of 300lb (136kg) breaking strain. If required, a lead weight of 4–6oz (113–170g) may be slipped onto the main line trace. As an added precaution, the main line is often doubled before attaching it to the top swivel by means of a carefully tied half-blood knot.

A hook length of 200lb (91kg) breaking strain is generally quite adequate for blues, but the additional strength ensures that the wire will not be bitten through should you accidentally encounter a large porbeagle or even a stray mako. All of the equipment used, particularly the ancillaries such as swivels and links, should be of 'big game' quality and continue to function effectively under extreme stress.

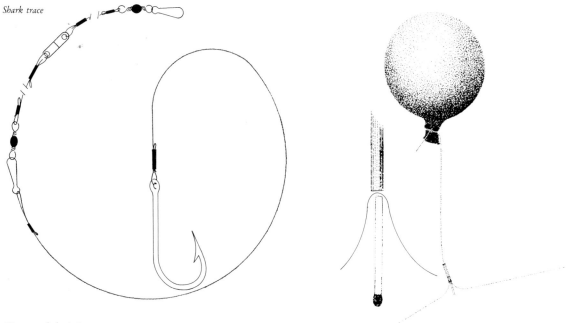

Shark trace

Balloon rig

Ground baiting

Before starting to fish you must attract the shark to the bait. This is done by means of a form of ground baiting called 'rubby-dubby'. It is a most disgusting mixture of fish, fish oil and bran. Stay well upwind of the concoction if you have any tendency towards sea-sickness. The recipe consists of eight to ten mackerel or herring, two cupfuls of fish oil and two to three cupfuls of bran. Dice the fish into small cubes and either mince or pound it into a watery pulp. Place the mixture in a bucket and add the oil and the bran. As they say in all the best cook books — then stir to taste! When ready, the rubby-dubby is poured into a perforated sack, such as an onion sack, and hung over the stern. The sack should weigh about six to eight pounds when it is first set in position. The boat is set drifting and the slap and wash of the waves and the swell releases oils and fish particles. The oil spreads out over the surface while the denser particles sink down into the tide. Some skippers use two or even three rubby-dubby sacks, placed strategically over the stern, port and starboard, to create a really strong scent trail. A well-filled sack should last about an hour. When changing sacks be particularly careful not to break the trail — have the second sack firmly secured and releasing its malodorous oils before retrieving the used sack.

Since shark can only scent upstream, it is vitally important that the scent trail is carefully set. It is really a job for the experienced skipper and may involve the judicious use of wind, tide and at times the engine. Ideally the trail should be laid against and across the run of the tide so that a broad slick is formed, both down and across the tide.

Fishing the blue shark

Mackerel are normally used as bait and there are two standard methods of mounting the fish. In the first, wire is run through the fish from head to tail using a baiting needle, and the shank is pulled through until the point and barb are protruding from the fish's flank, adjacent to the gill cover. The tail is lashed to the wire using strong thread or nylon. The second and simpler method involves a full fillet of mackerel taken from behind the head to the tail. The hook is passed through the fillet twice and the tail portion is again tied to the wire trace. Be sure to remove the tail and fins from the bait as this prevents it from spinning and twisting in the current.

Place the bait over the stern and free-line some 20 to 60m of line out from the boat. You must now attach a float. One of the most popular is a simple inflated balloon, attached by a short length of nylon to a matchstick which is tied to the main line. The matchstick is held in place by either a double hitch knot or by means of a simple plastic sleeve arrangement. When the shark takes the bait, the matchstick is either torn from its sleeve by the line pressure or is broken as it comes through the top eye of the rod.

It normally takes an hour or more before the first blue appears. Watch the oil slick exuded from the rubby-dubby sack and sooner or later you will see evidence of a shark; a disgruntled seagull suddenly taking off from the water, a large furrow across the calm oily slick, or best of all, the appearance of a shark fin just off the stern. The shark may initially miss your bait completely and head for the rubby-dubby bag, which he will attack if not taken on board immediately. Retrieve the sack as quickly as possible and draw in a bait towards the hunting shark. When he first takes the bait, he will mouth it for a short while before heading off on his first run. The balloon may skim across the surface or disappear from view altogether. If you are using the sleeve release system it may even pull free as the fish veers away from the boat. Lift the rod and allow the fish to run unimpeded but with your thumb hovering over the spool. If the line has gone slack, retrieve line until you are in contact with the shark, then permit him to continue his run.

After swimming for some 20 to 30m, the shark will stop to rearrange the bait in his mouth so that it may be swallowed head first. As in tope fishing, it is recommended to strike on the second run, but for mouth-hooked fish it is best to strike earlier — at the end of the initial run. To strike a shark, have the clutch tension set, put the reel in gear and retrieve line until the rod is horizontal to the surface; lift the rod firmly backwards, it is often necessary to do this a second time to really drive home the hook. If the fish has not faltered after an initial run of 30m or more, assume that he has reorientated the bait on the move, and strike.

The fish will then make a second, often longer, run but will soon tire. As soon as your quarry slackens his pace, apply pressure and, using the rod as a fulcrum, pump the fish back towards the boat until he takes another run against the drag. Blue shark are not particularly strong fighters and a sixty-pounder (27kg) can often be subdued in ten minutes or less.

Landing and tagging
When you have the fish at the side of the boat, move back from the gunwale and slacken off the drag. The skipper, wearing strong gardening gloves, will then catch the trace and steady the fish for landing. As part of a national research programme on the migration patterns of blue shark the skippers of many Irish boats have volunteered to tag all fish caught and return them alive to the water. Some prefer to tag their fish in the dorsal fin, while they are still in the water, and then snip the wire as near to the hook as possible. Irish shark tags are large objects similar to those used for ear-tagging cattle. A special applicator containing the two halves of the tag is slipped over the fin and once closed, the two sections are inseparably plugged together.

If the shark is to be brought on board it is either gaffed or tailed. Some authorities maintain that serious damage can be done to the internal organs of shark when they are removed from the buoyant supportive medium in which they live. If you intend to release your catch and wish him well, it is best to do so while the fish is still in the water. Use a hook which will quickly rust and cause little discomfort to the shark, once free. To release a mouth-hooked shark, pull back on his nose and insert a block of wood as a gag, cut out the hook by nicking the skin adjacent to the shank and pulling it free with a pliers or forceps. If the fish is deeply hooked, wait until he is well and truly dead before attempting to operate. Beware of reflex actions, for the primitive nervous system can function long after the heart has stopped beating.

Porbeagle shark
The porbeagle (*Lamna nasus*), also known as the herring or mackerel shark, is a strong, thick-bodied fish, brownish grey on the back with white undersides. It is a ferocious looking beast but is not harmful. More tolerant of cold water than the blue, the porbeagle was once quite prolific during the autumn and early winter months as it harassed the shoals of spawning herring. It prefers rough, rocky ground and is often to be found in the vicinity of underwater pinnacles or ledges. The porbeagle will venture into shallow water (2–4fm; 4–8m), and around the rocky coasts of County Clare the

dorsal fin and heterocircle tail of the fish are often seen within 50 to 100m of the shore.

Porbeagle average between 5 to 10ft (1.5–3m) in length and rarely grow larger than 11½ft (3.5m). They are a thickset fish and generally weigh between 80 and 200lb (36–91kg). The current Irish record stands at 365lb (165.5kg) but any fish over 150lb (68kg) is considered a specimen.

In some countries the flesh of porbeagle is much prized and it is claimed that the ammonia in the muscle is quickly released once cooked, providing a meat similar in both taste and texture to veal. The liver, which in larger specimens can weigh 110lb (50kg), is used for the production of oil and the skin is tanned to form a supple leather.

Reproduction

Gravid (pregnant) female porbeagles may be encountered at any time of the year. They mature at 5ft (1.5m) and each female produces between one and four pups. The embryos are held free in the uterus (ovoviviparous) until the young are born. Once the original yolk mass has been absorbed, the embryos turn their attention to the unfertilised eggs which they greedily consume. The young are some 24in (60cm) in length when born.

Feeding and hunting

The adults hunt herring, mackerel, spurdog, cod, flatfish and squid; near pinnacles they also feed on the prolific shoals of pollack and coalfish. The eyes of the porbeagle are proportionately larger than those of the blue and they are accredited with far superior eyesight.

Fishing for porbeagle

To tackle porbeagle with confidence, your equipment will need to be appreciably stronger than that used for blues. Porbeagle are immensely strong fish and a hundred-pounder may take well over thirty minutes to bring to the side of the boat. They have long lanceolate teeth, which bear tiny secondary cups in the adult. The powerful jaws and sharp teeth can make short work of weak traces and it is imperative to use wire with a breaking strain well in excess of 200lb (91kg). A 50–60lb (22.5–27kg) class rod will suffice but the reel should contain a minimum of 450m of 60–80lb (27–36kg) Dacron.

Porbeagle are attracted by rubby-dubby trails (see page 359) but they often require a more substantial appetiser and it is common practice to 'chum' when porbeagling. The chum should consist of substantial cubes of mackerel or herring measuring 2.5cm or more. If float fishing for porbeagle, you will need to fish at depths of 10 to 15fm (20–30m) and a 4–8oz (113–230g) spiral lead should be slipped onto the trace. They are more suspicious by nature than blues and you should use a small float; it may also be necessary to split open the bait and stitch the hook inside using strong cotton or wire. Be sure to leave the point and barb exposed. The wire trace, containing two or three large, good quality swivels, is arranged in the same manner as that shown for blues (see page 359).

Trolling

A more effective way of consistently locating large porbeagle is by trolling. Developed by my good friend Kevin Linnane, this method works best near underwater pinnacles where porbeagle gather to feed on the resident fish stocks. These shark seem to segregate into size groups following maturity and a given mark will provide porbeagle of a surprisingly consistent size. Perhaps this adaptation is similar to that shown in freshwater pike where the 'hotspots' also provide pike of a consistent size range. In the case of pike, fish outside of the acceptable range are considered either a threat or a potential food source! Perhaps the same is true of porbeagle.

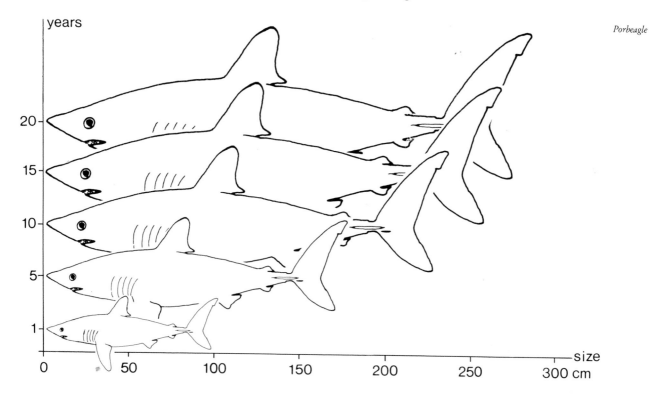

Porbeagle

A specific trolling rig has been developed by Kevin. The hooks are inserted into the mackerel as shown and the double hook acts as a form of keel. The lead ensures that the trolled bait is kept below the surface. Teasers are used in conjunction with the trolling rig and these consist of six to eight mackerel which have had their backbone removed, tied by their heads to a 30m nylon rope. They skutter, slap and bang on the surface some 20m ahead of the trolled baits and simulate a small shoal of mackerel feeding on the surface. The idea behind the teaser is to attract the porbeagle to the surface, allow him to snap off one or two fish, retrieve the teaser line and present him with the trolled bait.

When trolling, sharks take the bait with a ferocious bang and immediately dive down, hooking themselves in the process. The reel is not left on ratchet with the spool free, for this is to court disaster; rather the drag is set at 10-12lb (4.5-5.5kg) pressure. This may seem rather light but if the pressure is too strong, the fish will easily break the main line on its first dive. Should the porbeagle decide to head home with his prize, the initial run may revert to a 10 to 15fm (20-30m) dive. In this instance the strain on the main line is enormous, for not alone must it contend with 100 to 150lb (45.5-68kg) of powerful diving shark but also with the pressure of the tide or the great belly of line which is formed; only tighten the drag gradually as the speed of the fish begins to slacken. Having reached the bottom, the shark may dive about in erratic circles seeking to throw the hook. The angler should avoid the temptation to race around the decks after the shark but should fight it from either the stern or the bow, so that he can keep the line clear of the propeller or keel band.

As mentioned previously, large porbeagle, up to 145lb (66kg), were taken from the shore by Jack Shine during the early sixties. I am not aware of any recent captures from the shore, but the fish are still there. In 1987 two friends and I were visited by a majestic porbeagle while rock fishing from a mark just north of the Cliffs of Moher, where trolling for porbeagle was first attempted. The fish stayed with us for several minutes, patrolling up and down a definite contour line not 60m from the shore. We had noticed an inordinate amount of grilse jumping that evening and who knows, perhaps the porbeagle has a more discerning palate than was originally thought!

Porbeagle trolling rig

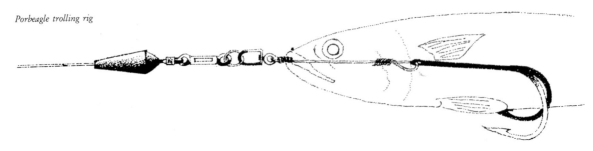

The low throb of the engine is masked only by the excited chatter of voices and the skipper's well-practised patter as we head on a south-easterly course past the Old Head of Kinsale. On our port side I can just make out the village of Oysterhaven and the indented coastline stretching northwards towards Cork Harbour.

The hot July sun breaks through the ceiling of dark purple cloud and dulls the edge of the fresh south-easterly breeze. The skipper looks up anxiously and remarks that air temperatures would need to rise a little higher if we are to be sure of a good day at the blues. Fervent prayers are offered up and many rash pacts are secretly made with the gods, but to no avail. Our brief sunny spell quickly disappears and we are back to sombre skies. Amongst the passengers, at least, spirits and expectations run high.

After steaming for a further ten minutes the skipper cuts the engine and the boat begins to drift. Feathers are lowered over the side but mackerel are difficult to find. Two more changes of location are called for before we encounter good quality mackerel in reasonable numbers. Twenty minutes later a fish box is half-filled with prime bait and we are on our way south, deep into the Celtic Sea.

Knowing little about navigation, I never cease to be impressed by the experienced skipper's uncanny ability to locate, time after time, his favourite marks and drifts. As we move along Paul expertly blends the essential rubby-dubby. Two of my friends, inexperienced in the ways of the sea, had insisted, despite my best efforts to dissuade them, on bacon, egg and sausage for breakfast. This fatal error is now beginning to tell. They high-tail it to the stern of the boat but even here the breeze carries the none too delicate whiff of oily mackerel, bran and fish oil deep into their sensitive nostrils. They both turn a strange pale colour but are slow to admit their discomfort and unaware that sea sickness can hit,

without warning, even the most hardened of sailors.

It seems we have reached our mark, for the skipper has cut the engine, and Paul quickly lowers the first bag of rubby-dubby over the side. He has made up three bags, since each one will last little more than an hour. In addition to my two companions and myself, there is also a Dutch couple, Peter and Hester, on board. The three of us busy ourselves preparing tackle and discussing tactics with the skipper. My friends are now openly admitting their malaise and while Paul attempts to comfort them with words of sympathy, we fillet mackerel and prepare our baits.

My Dutch companions prove to be experienced deep sea anglers and they deftly split open their mackerel and remove the entrails and the back bone. Having nipped off the tail and fins to prevent the bait spinning, they sew the forged 10/0 hook inside the bait, taking care to leave the barb and point exposed. Under the expert direction of the skipper, I am advised that while the more tedious camouflaging of the hook may be required for more discerning shark such as porbeagle, a side of mackerel threaded onto the hook, tail first, and sewn with strong elastic thread is fine for blues. I follow my instructions to the letter and soon my balloon float and that of my companions are bobbing out on the surface of the sea some 20m apart.

My two friends have by this stage lost their breakfast and a good half of the previous evening's dinner over the side of the boat. Paul advises them to lie prostrate on the flat deck and as they do, I and my lineage are roundly and soundly abused and cursed for suggesting such a masochistic way of spending a full day of their well-earned holidays. I ignore the abuse and settle down to watch the red bobbing float, lying some 30m astern of the boat.

The fresh mackerel is lying about 5fm (10m) below the float and is slowly being drawn along by the pull of the drifting boat. Hopefully, it is

139

surrounded by the flavour of the rubby-dubby whose potent odour will range far and wide down the ever-increasing scent trail. I can just imagine the sub-surface scenario which is being played out some 2km or more downtide of the waiting baits.

A hungry blue shark patrolling just below the surface, eagerly hunts out the smell and taste of shoaling fish. He has not eaten since dawn when he encountered a small group of spurdog, two of which fell foul of his strong jaws and finely serrated triangular teeth. He is now truly hungry and willing to consider even the smallest offerings. He moves along smoothly, his nostrils flared to permit the maximum intake of water and his intricately programmed olfactory lobes are busy decoding the familiar essences of the upper ocean. His head moves to the left and a faint oily whiff is sensed. He reorientates and faces into the strong current, the full force of the boat's scent trail assaults his nostrils. The shark's body reacts, almost involuntarily, as the prehistoric predatory instincts, honed over the ages of pre-history to a superfine sensitivity, begin to take control. He flexes his strong muscles and the light cartilaginous skeleton is propelled along through the water at increasing speed towards the waiting shoal of fodder fish. As the smell strengthens, the shark's behaviour becomes more irrational, he is working himself into a frenzied merciless state, he lunges from side to side across the delicious stream devouring tiny morsels of fish....

A shark fin. I jump up from my perch on the hatch and shout excitedly. All eyes are now trained on the calm slick behind the boat. The rubby-dubby bag is quickly hauled aboard. Nothing appears for thirty long seconds. Did my over-fertile imagination create the ultimate illusion? I truly begin to wonder. There it is again! The distinctive tail is plain for all to see. Relief, quickly followed by just a tinge of disappointment, the shark is heading for the Dutchman's bait. I retrieve my balloon and bait.

The skipper moves lithely across the deck and takes up position near the anxious Peter. He hands him a butt strap which is quickly draped around his waist. Rod in hand he waits for the next phase of the drama to unfold. He releases the spool of the great multiplier as the float moves across the slick, slowly at first but quickly gaining momentum. The shark strips about 40m from the reel. His pace begins to slacken. Peter engages the spool and strikes. The great fish is away on a second, more determined, run. The skipper murmurs some low key advice, the clutch setting is tightened slightly and the fight is on. The shark makes three long runs, pausing at the end of each. As he begins to slow down, experience shows and the confident Dutchman pumps the fish hard towards the boat, each time gaining just a little extra ground.

Eventually the exhausted shark is alongside the boat. The Dutchman moves back across the deck, releases the clutch setting in case of an emergency and leaves the rest to the skipper and Paul.

In the excitement, even my two erstwhile companions forget their predicament and, having arisen from the dead, drag themselves to the edge of the gunwale. With a gloved hand the skipper grabs hold of the strong wire trace and steadies the fish. Paul holds the tail while I attempt to slip a rope noose over it. In the tossing boat it is more difficult than might be imagined and twice the rope fails to slip around the base of the tail. Third time lucky, and the shark is secured. Quickly he is hauled aboard. The skipper expertly removes the large hook from the lower jaw while Paul prepares and checks the tag applicator. With a brief pause for a triumphant photograph, the 80lb (36kg) fish is tagged and released, hopefully unharmed, for the fish was less than five minutes on board the boat. As my companion re-baits, I decide that a carefully secured whole mackerel might be more effective. Good-naturedly the skipper tosses me a fresh bait

140

but it is obvious that he is just a little peeved at my decision.

One-and-a-half hours and two rubby-dubby changes later, I too am beginning to believe that the change of bait presentation was superfluous. The wind has strengthened considerably and my two friends are by now beside themselves with a mixture of grief, anger and self-pity. Their doleful cries ring in my ears as Paul patiently explains to them that there is no way the boat can return to port. I am feeling guilty, uneasy and if I were totally honest with myself, just a smidgen sea sick!

As I watch, my red float disappears completely from view and great folds of line are quickly stripped from my reel. With the reel screeching as it has never done before, I lift the rod and disengage the ratchet. I can sense the incredible surging power and confidence of my quarry as he accelerates confidently with the tide; one hundred, two hundred metres of line — the skipper is beside himself with excitement. 'A porbeagle, a porbeagle, it has to be, a porbeagle,' he rasps into my ear. With the powerful rod firmly set in the butt cap which is now garlanded around my waist, I breathlessly await instructions. My pulse is racing and I can feel my heart thumping out its adrenaline-ridden messages deep inside my chest.

'He's slowing ... easy now ... easy now ... engage the reel. Strike!' the skipper's voice is at fever pitch. Over two hundred pounds (91kg) of firm, solid muscle takes off on a second run but this time heads straight for the boat. Frantically I back away from the gunwale, madly retrieving line. The fish accelerates and dives down, down, down. With a sickening wrench I am in contact with him for a second time. The shock wrenches me from the hatch but the skipper's powerful hands grasp my shoulders and force me back down on the makeshift seat. The fish is right under the boat and circling incessantly around and around and around. My first reaction is to follow his passage by walking the decks after him, but the skipper restrains me. 'Fight him from the stern,' he orders.

Twenty-five minutes later and I am utterly exhausted. My back aches, my arms ache and my groin feels as if it has been cruelly speared. The porbeagle is still circling below. I am just about to hand the rod over to the skipper when I sense a change of mood. The fish is definitely tiring. I pump hard and the shark moves slowly towards the surface. Five agonising minutes later and I have him beside the boat.

The skipper peers over the side and shouts: 'It's huge. Close to 200lb.' Images of specimen fish and special merit awards flash across my mind. The skipper steadies the trace. Paul stands by with the tailing noose. The absolute dregs of my adrenaline supplies rush to my weary heart as I slowly and anxiously peer over the gunwale. A huge, thickset, dark brown back peers up at me. Just at that instant the shark makes one last desperate effort to escape. The trace is torn from the skipper's hand in a welter of foam as the fish lunges under the boat. My clutch is loose and line peels freely off the reel, but the fish has learned his lesson and he stays shallow, and the line, sizzling across the keel band, is cut to ribbons. Fish, trace and hook disappear into the depths.

There is utter silence on board the boat. Anxious faces turn towards me but I am too numbed and exhausted to speak. The only sound to break the silence is the slap of the waves and the loud contented snoring of my eldest companion, now soundly asleep in the wheel house. The skipper turns the boat about and heads for port.

Skate and ray

Skate, ray and their relatives are grouped by biologists under the general, but very descriptive, term of 'batoids'. Their lineage is shorter than that of other selachians, but fossil members of the group have been traced back 130 million years to the upper Jurassic Age. The batoids can be subdivided further into five major groups: skate, ray, electric ray, sawfish and guitar fish.

Although displaying a great variety of different shapes and forms, these flattened shark have retained all the basic selachian characteristics: they mate and breed like shark, feed carnivorously like shark and their skeleton is formed from blocks of that most characteristically shark-like substance: cartilage. Their bodies have adapted to a slow-moving existence on the ocean floor. Gone are the laterally sited gill slits of the pelagic shark and in their place are twin, valve-operated spiracles. Dorsally placed, these permit water to be drawn past the gills and expelled through the gill clefts on the ventral surface. Batoids' teeth are designed for crushing, and range in shape from spikey prongs set on a broad base to flattened, rounded teeth set in a tightly arranged mosaic pattern.

They are known to range in size from tiny ray, with little more than a 2–3in (5–7.5cm) wingspan, to the giant ray (*Manta birostris*) measuring 6.5m or more across the wings and weighing 3000 pounds (1361kg).

Skate

In addition to the common skate (*Raja batis*) there are two other species which occur in Irish waters: the white skate (*Raja alba*) and the long-nosed skate (*Raja oxyrinchus*). These latter two species are not very common and may be caught using the tackle and techniques described below for taking the common skate.

Endangered species

Although never a prolific species in the same sense as ling or conger, the common skate was frequently encountered by deep sea anglers until the mid-seventies, when the population collapsed. The cause was simple and straightforward: overfishing. In 1965 the commercial harvest of common skate from the Irish Sea stood at 900 tonnes. By 1975 this had plummeted to 190 tonnes. Once the stable door was well and truly shut, all the agencies responsible for its welfare and survival rushed into action. Legislation was enacted on both sides of the Irish Sea and the endangered species was given the protection of the law — about ten years too late! When managing localised stocks of long-lived, late-maturing species which also have an extremely low fecundity rate, it is important to remember that even moderate angling pressure may endanger such populations. But, the good news is that the conservation measures seem, at last, to be taking effect and there is every indication that stocks are very slowly improving. A voluntary ban by anglers on the killing of skate has undoubtedly contributed to this improvement. Perhaps in five to ten years' time skate fishing may once again regain its once-held position as a major component of Irish deep sea angling. On that basis I consider it fitting to include a section on skate and their capture.

Maturation and spawning
Common skate are a very slow-growing fish and only reach sexual maturity at ten or eleven years of age and at a length of 4ft (120cm). Common skate are long-lived and can occasionally reach fifty years of age. They do not seem to undertake any form of spawning migration and it is now generally agreed that stocks are very localised. The females spawn between May and July, releasing a small number of very large eggs. Each embryo is contained in a horny capsule, often measuring 5in x 10in (13cm x 25cm), the true mermaid's purse. The gestation period varies between two and five months.

Skate

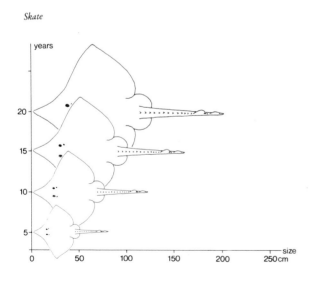

Thornback Ray

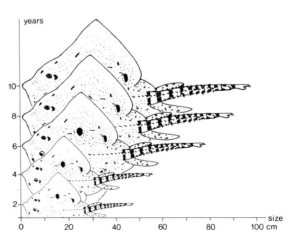

Skate may be encountered in the most unusual places. My first experience of skate fishing was not from a boat but from a deepwater pier. Many years ago, while holidaying in Scotland, I found myself, one beautiful August evening, fishing the pier at Ullapool. Bait was scarce and I was forced to settle for a few rather anaemic looking fillets of not very fresh mackerel. Having diced these into usable portions, I settled down for a quiet evening's fishing. I was using a light beachcaster 15lb (6.5kg) line and 25lb (11kg) shock leader, on a multiplier reel. My bottom rig consisted of a size 4/0 single hook and a running leger, which I reckoned was quite adequate to handle anything I was likely to encounter.

How wrong I was. The pier was largely deserted and apart from the squawk of the occasional gull and the distant hum of traffic, no other noise broke the tranquil silence. Then out of the blue a large, gleaming, maroon Volvo estate arrived on the pier. To say that the driver was a giant is an understatement; a good 2m in height and weighing at least 25 stone (160kg), he totally blocked the setting sun as he stood before me, critically examining the teenager and his tackle. I must have passed muster, for with a slight nod of the head, he simply said: 'Evening mate, not much doing, eh!' I agreed. He donned the most incredibly fluorescent jumper, festooned with creamy white badges, each bearing a black number. I was later to learn that these signified his improving status as a 'big caster'. Sported proudly across his clavicle was a badge bearing red lettering with the legend 209m. From the car he produced an immaculate set of matched tackle and, quickly assembling a bottom rig similar to my own, he produced a portion of beautifully fresh squid and a box of king ragworm. He mounted half a king rag on the hook and tipped it with a cube of squid. Standing well clear of all obstructions, he executed an exquisite pendulum cast. That lead flew so far and so fast I could not even have guessed

where it landed. But my cocky cockney friend left me in no doubt: 'Not bad. 'Bout 180 yards. Just on the bank.' At this I really began to feel intimidated, he obviously knew his marks. We settled down in silence to our vigil.

With all these distractions, I had paid little attention to my own modest rod which was set on ratchet and free spool. Sitting on a conveniently located capstan, I noticed the tip start to bend in a slow but purposeful arc. Lifting the rod from its rest, I could feel nothing except a heavy drag. The ratchet began to tick, releasing line. I waited some seconds more and then struck. Solid resistance. I struck again, this time a good deal harder. The unexpected happened, the line went completely slack as the fish moved against the run of the tide. The cockney was beside me in a flash. 'Small doggie,' he announced, knowledgeably. I did not dare challenge this definitive assertion.

My 'doggie' came to rest under the pier. I retrieved line and began to apply pressure. The fish came very quietly and very easily. Suddenly he realised that all was not right with its world and arched away to my left. I do not exaggerate when I say that he very nearly toppled me into the water. The astonished cockney's only comment: 'Bloody 'ell, mate!' The fish was by this time near the surface and in the gathering darkness his great wings kited out of the water not 20m from us. It was an enormous skate. The cockney estimated it to be well over 100lb (45.5kg), and who was I to argue? It was obviously tired of playing games and intent on reaching the bottom as fast as 'skately' possible. He dived, tore line off the reel and disappeared into the murky depths. Somewhere between the surface and the ocean bed his thorny skin clipped the shock leader and parted it like thread — 'ping' the severed line came billowing back towards us.

The cockney grabbed his rod, winched back in his rig, re-baited with a piece of *my* mackerel and lobbed the weight out into the darkening channel.

'They travel in pairs you know,' he said. There was a horrendous squawk, the rod jumped and he was fast into a very irate and very large herring gull. What a mess. He played that bird for almost five minutes before landing him. Luckily the hook had torn free and was buried in the feathers. The cockney covered the great bird's head and beak with an immaculate Barbour jacket and expertly snipped the hook free while I struggled to hold the bird. By the time he had finished, the lining of the coat was in ribbons, lacerated by the bird's strong and efficient beak. Disgusted, he threw his tackle and the remains of his new coat back into the rear of his bright red car. At last I found my voice. 'Not off already, are you? Gulls often travel in pairs too.' With a loud, clearly spoken expletive, he banged the driver's door and roared off into the gathering darkness, leaving me to ponder on what might have been!

Fishing for skate

Adult common skate have been recorded from the shallows into depths of 250fm (500m) or more. However, they are most common in 20 to 50fm (40-100m) of water. The average weight of rod-caught skate is between 80 and 150lb (36-68kg) but the Irish record skate stands at 221lb (100kg). Exceptional specimens have been known to reach close on 400lb (182kg).

A battle with a large skate ultimately reverts to a test of strength between the angler and the fish. They may lack the swift sizzling runs of the porbeagle, but their powerful throbbing dives from surface to bottom can set the senses tingling and the adrenaline levels soaring.

Skate may be encountered over almost any type of ground: sand, mud, gravel or rock, but they seem to prefer rough mixed ground with a good sweep of tide. Despite their ungainly appearance, they are efficient foragers and may have a wide variety of food in their stomachs: cod, ling, pollack, whiting, hake, gurnard, squid, flatfish. They seem to follow a pattern when quartering an area and will appear on specific marks at definite times of the tide.

Tackle

To tackle skate you will require a 50-60lb (22.5-27kg) class hollow fibreglass rod with plenty of power and a large multiplier reel containing 400 to 500m of 50-80lb (22.5-36kg) Dacron. Skate are normally taken fishing at anchor with a running leger. The wire incorporated in the hook length should be 150-200lb (68-91kg) breaking strain and the hook size will vary from 6/0 to 10/0, depending on the size of the bait. The lead should be attached by a weak 20-30lb (9-13.5kg) length of 'rotten bottom' so that it may be snapped off if it tangles during the course of the fight.

Baiting

Bait consists of mackerel or herring. A whole small fish or a side of a larger oily fish is used. Half mackerel are also good bait, particularly the head portion with the viscera still attached. The bait is mounted tail first in much the same way as for blue sharks and it is bound to the wire trace using elastic thread. Mackerel heads are hooked through the eye sockets or through the head between the eyes, leaving the barb and point exposed.

When baited, let the trace down carefully so that you know when you have touched bottom. Use adequate lead to hold bottom and try to remain in contact with your sinker and trace all of the time. Bites are difficult to detect and may be missed if there is slack line between the weight and the rod tip. As the boat rises and falls on the waves, move your rod tip in unison with the waves so that the lead remains stationary.

When a skate finally flops down on the bait and mouths it gently, you will feel no more than a series of gentle tugs. Wait until he moves off with the bait. The slipping clutch should be carefully pre-set so as to take account of his initial frantic dive.

Striking

The strike is similar to that described for conger. With the rod horizontal to the waves, lift with all of your might and attempt to pull the skate free of the bottom. If the fish shifts, keep him coming, pumping him towards the surface. Sooner or later, however, he will make a frantic dive towards the seabed. If he reaches bottom, he can exert an amazing degree of suction and stick to the bottom with surprising tenacity and force. Keep a steady, firm strain and he will eventually pull loose. He may make a further three or four dives, but each time you will notice that he is weakening. Once you have succeeded in forcing his snout up above the bottom, the rushing tide will help to pull him free.

If your skate runs with the tide, you may have great difficulty pumping his great flat bulk back towards the boat. Pace yourself and make sure not to exert too much energy on the initial stages of the battle royal. When the skate is beside the boat, nip the wire trace as near to the hook as possible or cut the hook free if it is near the front of his mouth.

The cockney was right about one thing, skate do travel in pairs, a male and a female. Once you have released your skate, clip on a fresh hook length and re-bait quickly, for you stand a good chance of taking the second skate. The smaller of the two is invariably the male, but he often provides a far livelier and more exciting battle than his lethargic mate.

Thornback ray

Distinctive features

The thornback ray (*Raja clavata*) is a most distinctive creature with its dermal denticles fused into large, curved, thorn-like spines. These thorns are set in raised, swollen bases which lie on the dorsal surface and tail of the fish. Confusion may arise with some specimens, for at times these spines may be stubby and worn or even missing. The most distinctive features of the thornback are the dark black bandings on its tail.

Other species

Other common species of Irish ray include blonde ray (*Raja brachyura*), homelyn (*Raja montagui*) and the cuckoo ray (*Raja naevus*). Amongst the less common ray are the beautiful undulate (*Raja undulata*), which is pretty well confined to Tralee Bay, County Kerry, and the very special sting ray (*Dasyatis pastinaca*), which we shall deal with separately in the following section.

Location

The thornback is found over clear bottoms of sand, gravel or mud and at depths ranging from less than a fathom to 140fm (< 2m–280m). It moves close inshore in May and June and feeds on a broad variety of organisms including crabs, shrimps, prawns, worms, shellfish, sandeels and a range of demersal fish. It is particularly fond of shallow sand banks situated at the entrance to large estuaries or bays.

Maturation and spawning

Thornback mate throughout the year and the oviparous females spawn between 70 and 170 eggs, depending on their size. Each embryo is encased in a horny purse measuring some 3in x 2in (6.5cm x 5cm). The gestation period is four to five months. Males mature at seven years of age and at a length of 20 to 32in (50–80cm), females at nine years of age and a length of 26 to 37in (65–95cm). Like their close relative, the skate, they are a relatively slow-growing, late-maturing species but their high fecundity rate makes populations more resistant to overfishing. However, when heavily harvested, their average size quickly falls.

Boat fishing

Most fishing for thornback is carried out at anchor from small inshore boats or dinghies over shallow sandy banks. The flood tide is often best, with more and more ray appearing as the flow strengthens. The fish range in size from 4 to 8lb (2–3.5kg) and there is always a chance of a fifteen- to twenty-pounder. They grow to over 40lb (18kg) but specimens of 20lb (9kg) are comparatively rare off these inshore marks.

Tackle

Because of the clean bottom and shallow depths, light gear can be used to good effect. Bass tackle is ideal; a light 11ft (3.5m) rod, 15lb (6.5kg) main line and a medium-sized multiplier will deal with all eventualities. On some sheltered marks it is possible to use a salmon spinning rod, fixed-spool reel and 12-15lb (5.5-6.5kg) main line. On such tackle a good-sized kiting thornback can put up a respectable scrap.

Terminal tackle involves a 30-35lb (13.5-16kg) shock leader and a running leger rig with an 18in (45cm) hook length of 40-50lb (18-22.5kg) monofilament. Wire is not required, although the leader and hook length should be regularly inspected for abrasion. Thornback have flat grinding teeth which can pulverise soft metal hooks. You are well advised to use a strong stainless steel or cadmium coated size 4/0 to 6/0 hook.

Baiting and striking

The normal bait for ray is a strip of fresh mackerel or herring, ragworm or squid. They are very discerning at times and the bait should, if possible, be fresh from the sea. Some friends and I have recently found that estuarine ray are particularly fond of soft or peeler crab, and I have no doubt that they would also work well on inshore marks. As in skate fishing, the bait should be kept on the bottom and sufficient lead should be used to ensure that the bait stays put.

As the ray flops down on the bait the angler will sense two to three sharp tugs and a slow draw as the fish moves off with the bait. It may take three or four excruciating minutes before that first run, and the angler should be patient. Give a good sharp strike and lift the fish clear of the bottom. As you pump him back towards the boat he may spread his wings flat against the run of the tide. This provides him with great torque, but if you are patient you can winch him slowly towards the side of the boat, even on very light tackle.

Landing

Do not attempt to net or hand-hold the fish, as the sharp spines will make short work of skin or netting. A sharp gaff is the best instrument to use if you intend retaining the fish. Insert the gaff into the wing just behind the cartilaginous ridge which runs along its outer edge.

When on board you must subdue your fish quickly and humanely. Turn him over on his back and administer a few short, sharp blows to the snout. **Take care not to miss and punch a hole in the bottom of the boat in your enthusiasm — it has happened. Store your fish in a fish**

box to avoid sliming the deck or accidents from those sharp spines.

Storing and cooking

Ray flesh contains high concentrations of ammonia and is revolting if eaten fresh. However, if bled and hung for a few days it provides superb meat. To bleed the fish, cut through the gills using a sharp long-bladed knife. Next run the blade around the abdominal cavity and remove the viscera. Cut down deep to separate the wing roots from the body. This severs a further set of main blood vessels. Wash the wings clean in salt water, and when you get home hang them in a garage or shed for two days. Be sure that your storage area is not too hot and that it is bluebottle- and fly-proof. After two days you may freeze the wings or cook them 'fresh'. If you intend freezing the ray, do not wash it before freezing. To skin 'fresh' or thawed ray, dip it in hot water before cooking and the hard skin and spines will curl away.

Shore fishing

Shore fishing for thornback is a very exciting but undependable sport. During calm, warm, sultry weather in May and June they may visit the beaches at irregular intervals, usually at night. To take full advantage of such occurrences you must cast well out (80–120m) and fish with really fresh bait. As in the case of skate, thornback travel in pairs and if you catch one you stand a good chance of taking a second fish. The tackle described for boat fishing will double for shore fishing, as you will rarely need to use a lead much heavier than 4oz (113g). The most productive baits are peeler or soft crab and oily fish such as mackerel or herring.

Deepwater pier fishing for thornback is frequently more productive than beach fishing. The ray lie over a muddy, sandy bottom and can be caught at specific stages of the tide over quite a prolonged season. They also penetrate deep into larger estuaries when the freshwater discharge is low and the salinity levels correspondingly high.

Sting ray

Distinctive features

A member of an ancient and varied group of ray, the sting ray (*Dasyatis pastinaca*) is one of the most feared fish species throughout the world. They vary considerably in size, from the tiny Atlantic species (*Dasyatis sabina*) measuring no more than 20in (51cm) in width to the giant *Dasyatis centroura* which can reach 5ft (1.5m) in width and a length of over 10ft (3m).

The ventral sting or stings located on the dorsal surface of its tail have been used for defence and nefarious purposes:

Spears tipped by one or more stingers have been used by Malayans, natives of many Pacific islands, hunters in South and Central American Indian tribes, and Australian aborigines. Frightful whips made from the thorny, stinger-bearing tails of an African type of sting ray have been seen by explorers along the Congo and in tropical West Africa. In Ceylon, sting ray tails were used, until recent times, as whips for punishing criminals. They were also used in the Seychelles Archipelago of the Indian Ocean to keep wives in order!

(McCormick, Allen and Young, 1963)

The single, serrated, dorsally located spine on the tail of *Dasyatis pastinaca* is venomous and although not fatal, it may cause local paralysis. Should you suffer a wound, let it bleed for a few moments, to flush out as much poison and sand as possible. Wash the wound thoroughly, apply a mild antiseptic and hightail it to the local doctor.

Reproduction
Unlike other ray, sting ray are viviparous and give birth to their six to nine pups during the summer months. The young are retained in their mother's uterus for a period of some four months prior to birth. It is known that males mature at 26–27in (65–70cm) and females at 28–30in (70–75cm).

Feeding
Sting ray feed on a selection of bottom-dwelling animals but the juveniles' diet is crustacean-based. The adults feed primarily on a mixture of larger crustaceans and fish.

Fishing for sting ray
Sting ray have been growing in importance as a sport fish in Britain for a number of years and I believe that once 'discovered' by Irish anglers they will quickly become a cult fish in much the same way as the smooth hound or the shad.

The sting ray is a large semi-pelagic creature reaching a maximum size of 70lb (32kg). A strong, fast-moving fish, it fights in much the same manner as a tope and when hooked in the shallows it will often leap clear of the water.

The sting ray is migratory, moving onto beaches and into warm shallow estuaries during the summer months but retreating into deeper water in autumn. It delights in tepid conditions and appreciable numbers will often invade a beach synchronously. Its distribution around Ireland is poorly known but sting ray are probably far more common than was once realised. They are to be found in good numbers along the south Wexford and Kerry coasts.

Boat fishing
They can be taken from either a small boat, fishing close inshore, or from the beach. When boat

fishing, move the craft close to the larger sand banks. When the tide is nearly full the sting-ray will be found basking on the summits of these thermal mounds of fine sand, in no more than a half to 2.5m of water. The fish are easily frightened and it often pays to row into position some 20 to 30 metres from your chosen bank.

Tackle

A light 15–20lb (6.5–9kg) class boat rod and a multiplier reel with 200 to 300m of 15–30lb (6.5–13.5kg) main line or a light bass-type 11ft (3.5m) beachcaster may be used. Use a straight running leger and a hook length of 3 to 4ft (90–120cm) of 30lb (13.5kg) nylon. Hook sizes can vary from 3/0 to 5/0 but as in the case of thornback, ensure that they are of good quality metal. The normal baits are ragworm, soft or peeler crab or mackerel strip.

Striking

For such a lethargic looking creature, a sting ray can take with quite a violent rush. Be sure to have your drag pre-set and strike the fish firmly after he has taken a few metres of line. He will generally take off on a great flurry of a run, frequently breaking the surface or leaving a deep furrow as he accelerates through the shallow water. You will find that a 15–20lb (6.5–9kg) sting ray may take quite a while to subdue and when you do get him next to the boat, be prepared for that final desperate dive.

Landing

Landing sting ray can be a dangerous business. Under no circumstances, no matter how committed you are to your conservation principles, attempt to snip the trace when the fish is lying beside the boat. He will quickly arch his tail and neatly plant his long serrated spine deep in your forearm.

Use a large landing net for fish up to 15lb (6.5kg) and a strong gaff for bigger specimens. Insert the gaff into the leading edge of the wing and hold the fish well clear of your body as you lift him on board. Throw a sack or old coat over the fish to subdue him, and pinning his tail firmly to the bottom of the boat, remove the hook. Keep the fish in the net or impaled on the gaff while you unhook him, then return your prize to the sea by inverting the net or disengaging the gaff with a sharp push.

Shore fishing

For shore fishing use similar tackle and traces to those described for use from inshore boats. In some locations a long cast may be required to reach distant bars or sandbanks. When you encounter such situations, be sure to have plenty of reserve line on the reel in case you hook a really large powerful specimen. When landing your ray, take extra care as before. The use of a long-handled gaff when securing ray from a flat beach is strongly recommended by many devotees of the sport.

Festooned with sharp, continuously growing teeth, this mako shark jaw is an awesome sight

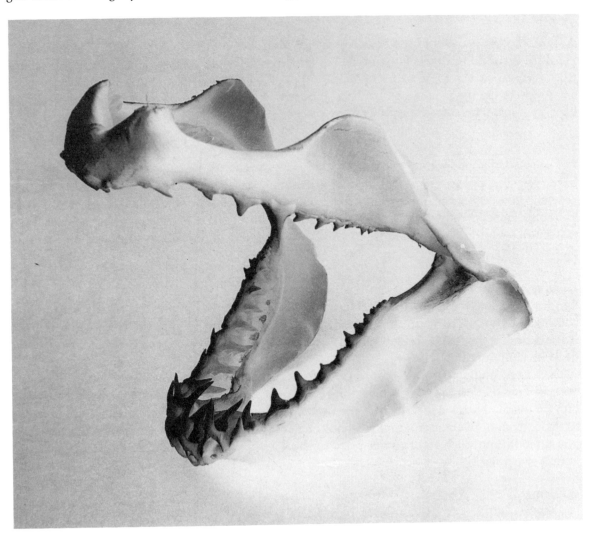

APPENDIX 2

Useful addresses

Central Fisheries Board
Balnagowan
Mobhi Boreen
Glasnevin
Dublin 9
Tel: (01) 379206

Bord Fáilte/Irish Tourist Board
Baggot Street Bridge
Dublin 2
Tel: (01) 765871

Department of Agriculture for Northern Ireland
Fisheries Division
Hut 5 Castle Grounds
Stormont
Belfast BT4 3TA
Tel: Belfast 63939

Foyle Fisheries Commission
8 Victoria Road
Derry BT47 2AB
Tel: (0504) 42100

Northern Ireland Tourist Board
River House
48 High Street
Belfast BT1 2DS
Tel: Belfast 31221

Shannon Regional Fisheries Board
Thomond Weir
Limerick
Tel: (061) 55171

South Western Regional Fisheries Board
1 Nevilles Terrace
Massey Town
Macroom
Co. Cork
Tel: (026) 41221

Southern Regional Fisheries Board
Anglesea Street
Clonmel
Co. Tipperary
Tel: (052) 23624

Eastern Regional Fisheries Board
Mobhi Boreen
Glasnevin
Dublin 9
Tel: (01) 379206

Northern Regional Fisheries Board
Station Road
Ballyshannon
Co. Donegal
Tel: (072) 51435

North Western Regional Fisheries Board
Abbey Street
Ballina
Co. Mayo
Tel: (096) 22788

Western Regional Fisheries Board
Weir Lodge
Earl's Island
Galway
Tel: (091) 63118/119/110

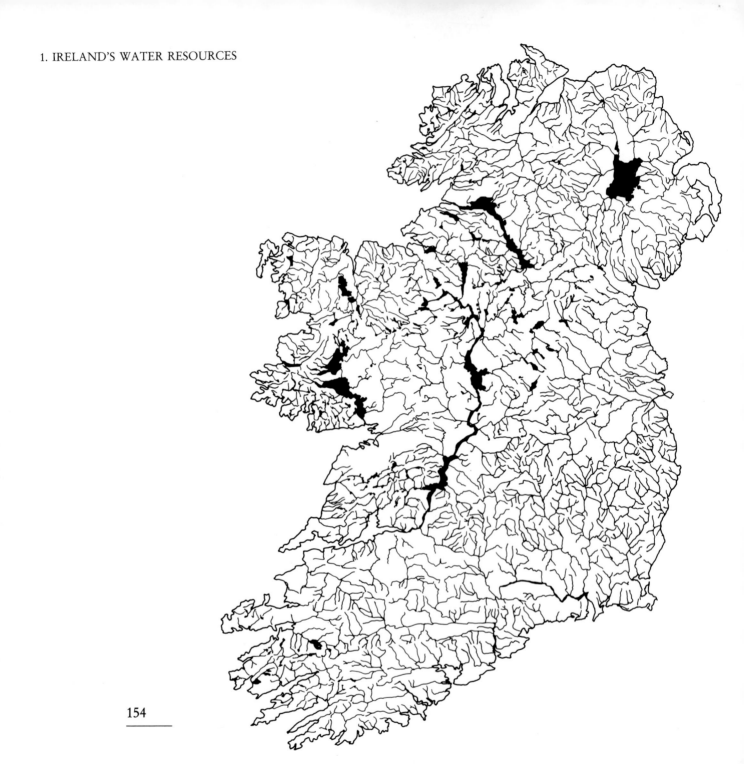

2. SEA ANGLING CENTRES

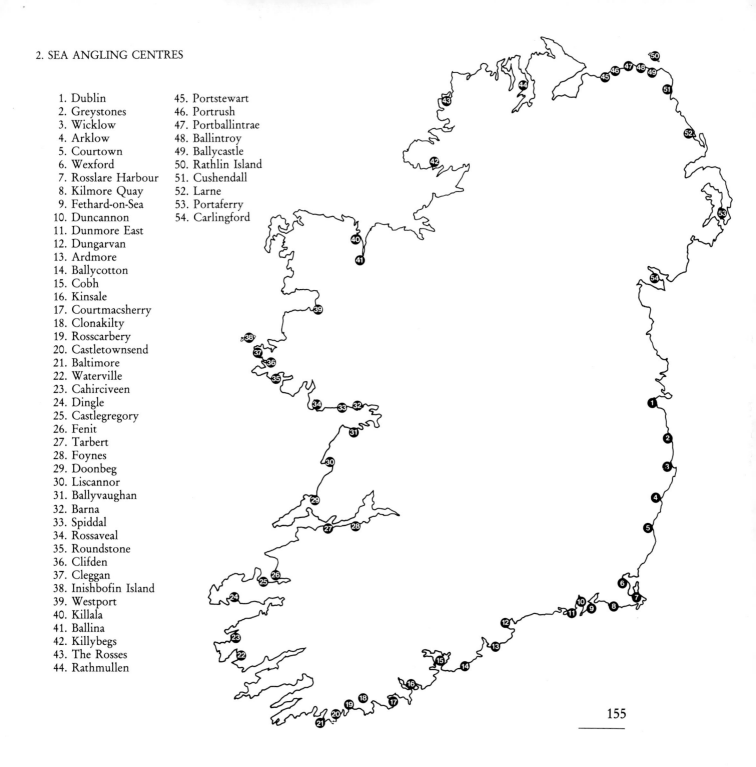

1. Dublin
2. Greystones
3. Wicklow
4. Arklow
5. Courtown
6. Wexford
7. Rosslare Harbour
8. Kilmore Quay
9. Fethard-on-Sea
10. Duncannon
11. Dunmore East
12. Dungarvan
13. Ardmore
14. Ballycotton
15. Cobh
16. Kinsale
17. Courtmacsherry
18. Clonakilty
19. Rosscarbery
20. Castletownsend
21. Baltimore
22. Waterville
23. Cahirciveen
24. Dingle
25. Castlegregory
26. Fenit
27. Tarbert
28. Foynes
29. Doonbeg
30. Liscannor
31. Ballyvaughan
32. Barna
33. Spiddal
34. Rossaveal
35. Roundstone
36. Clifden
37. Cleggan
38. Inishbofin Island
39. Westport
40. Killala
41. Ballina
42. Killybegs
43. The Rosses
44. Rathmullen
45. Portstewart
46. Portrush
47. Portballintrae
48. Ballintroy
49. Ballycastle
50. Rathlin Island
51. Cushendall
52. Larne
53. Portaferry
54. Carlingford

155

BIBLIOGRAPHY

Annual Reports of the Inland Fisheries Trust. (1951-80) IFT, Glasnevin, Dublin.

BENNETT, J. (1958) *Big-Game Angling.* Faber and Faber, London. 220pp

BRANDER, K. (1977) 'The management of the Irish Sea fisheries — a review.' Lab. leafl. MAFF. Direct. Fish. Res. Lowestoft. (36) 40pp

BRENNAN, D. (1965) *The Sea Angler Afloat and Ashore.* A. and C. Black Ltd, London. 346pp

(1974) *Bass.* Osprey Publishing Ltd, Berkshire. 48pp

(1974) *Skates and Rays.* Osprey Publishing Ltd, Berkshire. 48pp

CONNOLLY, P. L. (1986) *Aspects of the Biology of the Gurnard (Pices: Triglidae) from the Irish Sea.* Ph.D. thesis. National University of Ireland.

FITZMAURICE, P. (1974) 'Size distribution and food of thornback rays (*Raja clavata* L.) caught on rod and line on the Mayo Coast.' *Irish Fish. Invest.* Ser. B, no. 11, 18pp

GODDARD, JOHN (1977) *Big Fish from Salt Water — A Guide to the Tackle, Techniques, Species and Venues in British, European and African Waters.* Ernest Benn Ltd, London and Tonbridge. 244pp

GRAINGER, R.J.R. (1986) *Fisheries and Mariculture in the Irish Sea.* Department of the Marine, Dublin.

GRIFFITH, D. de G. (1971) 'Notes on the biology of the plaice (*Pleuronectes platessa* L.)' M.Sc. Thesis. Trinity College, Dublin.

GRIFFITH, D. de G. (1983) 'Living Marine Resources' in *A Profit and Loss Account of Science in Ireland.* Edited by Clinch, E.M. and Mollan, C. Royal Dublin Society, Ballsbridge, Dublin. 30-48

(1985) 'The biological basis of fisheries management — future scope for action' in *Ireland — The Atlantic — Exploitation of its Resources.* Proceedings of a conference held in Cork 14-15 Nov 1985. Sherkin Island Marine Station, Co. Cork. 57-66

HARDY, A. (Sir) (1956) *The Open Sea. Its Natural History.* Part One: The World of Plankton. Collins. 393pp

HARRIS, B. (1977) *The Guinness Guide to Saltwater Angling — Light Tackle Techniques for British Waters.* Guinness Superlatives Ltd, Middlesex. 238pp

Irish Sport Fishes — A Guide to their Identification. Central Fisheries Board, Dublin. 66pp

KENNEDY, M. (1954) *The Sea Angler's Fishes.* Hutchinson, London. 524pp

(1956) *Salt Water Angling.* Hutchinson, London. 376pp

KENNEDY, M. and FITZMAURICE, P. (1969) 'Age and growth of thick-lipped grey mullet (*Crenimugil labrosus*) in Irish waters.' *J. Mar. Biol. Ass. UK,* 49, 683-699

(1972) 'The biology of the bass (*Dicentrarchus labrax*) in Irish waters.' *J. Mar. Biol. Ass. UK,* 52, 557-559

LINNANE, K. (1974) *Sharks. The Osprey Anglers.* Edited by Clive Gammon. Osprey Publishing Ltd, Berkshire, England. 48pp

LINEAWEAVER, T. H. and BACUS, R. H. (1970) *The Natural History of Sharks.* Andre Deutsch Ltd, London. 256pp

McCORMICK, H. W., ALLEN, T. and YOUNG, CAPTAIN W. E. (1963) *Shadows in the Sea. The Sharks, Skates and Rays.* Sidgwick and Jackson, London. 415pp

MILLMAN, M. (1979) *Sea Angling Supreme.* Cassell Ltd, London. 157pp

MUUS, B. J. and DAHLSTROM, P. (1974) *Sea Fishes of Britain and North-Western Europe.* (Collins Guide) Collins, London. 244pp

QUERO, JEAN-CLAUDE (1984) *Les Poissons de Mer des Pêches Françaises.* Maquette Dominique et Philippe Lemonnier, Paris. 394pp

STOKER, H. (ed.) (1977) *Sea Angling with the Specimen Hunters — Big Fish Tactics of the Experts.* Ernest Benn Ltd, London and Tonbridge. 216pp

WENT, A.E.J. and KENNEDY, M. (1976) *List of Irish Fishes.* Stationery Office, Dublin. 47pp

INDEX